SHOPPING MATTERS 2

Englisch für Einzelhandelskaufleute

von Maria Elisabeth Köstler

Shopping Matters 2 wurde geplant und entwickelt von der Verlagsredaktion der Cornelsen und Oxford University Press GmbH & Co.

Verfasserin:	Maria Elisabeth Köstler, Wien
Verlagsredaktion:	Janan Barksdale
Redaktionelle Mitarbeit:	Andreas Goebel, Eleanor Toal, Fritz Preuss (wordlists)
Design / Herstellung:	Oxford Designers & Illustrators
Bildredaktion:	Uta Hübner
Umschlagfoto:	Comstock Fotoagentur

Erhältlich sind auch:
Audio-CD
Lehrerhandbuch

www.cornelsen.de

1. Auflage, 4. Druck 2008

Alle Drucke dieser Auflage sind inhaltlich unverändert
und können im Unterricht nebeneinander verwendet werden.

© 2001 Cornelsen & Oxford University Press GmbH & Co., Berlin.

Das Werk und seine Teile sind urheberrechtlich geschützt.
Jede Nutzung in anderen als den gesetzlich zugelassenen Fällen bedarf der
vorherigen schriftlichen Einwilligung des Verlages.
Hinweis zu den §§ 46, 52 a UrhG: Weder das Werk noch seine Teile dürfen ohne eine
solche Einwilligung eingescannt und in ein Netzwerk eingestellt oder sonst öffentlich
zugänglich gemacht werden.
Dies gilt auch für Intranets von Schulen und sonstigen Bildungseinrichtungen.

Druck: CS-Druck CornelsenStürtz, Berlin

ISBN 978-3-464-02595-6

 Inhalt gedruckt auf säurefreiem Papier aus nachhaltiger Forstwirtschaft.

Vorwort

Shopping Matters ist ein neues, zweibändiges Lehrwerk für Einzelhandelskaufleute, die am Berufsschulunterricht oder an betrieblichen Fortbildungsmaßnahmen teilnehmen. Das Werk basiert auf den Lehrplänen der Berufsschulen. Der zweite Band des Lehrwerks baut auf dem ersten Band auf, kann aber auch allein verwendet werden.

Shopping Matters Band 2 besteht – wie auch Band 1 – aus 12 Units sowie einer Übungseinheit zur englischen Geschäftskorrespondenz. In jeder Unit werden die Lernenden in berufsbezogenen Situationen mit allen wesentlichen Aspekten des Englischen vertraut gemacht. Es ist möglich, einzelne Units auszulassen, jedoch wird empfohlen, wann immer Zeit und Lehrpläne es erlauben, die gegebene Reihenfolge einzuhalten, um einen kontinuierlichen Aufbau des Fachvokabulars und der grammatikalischen Strukturen zu gewährleisten.

Shopping Matters bietet die Möglichkeit eines handlungsorientierten wie auch eines praxisbezogenen Unterrichts. Die Lernenden schulen aktiv ihre Sprechfertigkeit in Rollenspielen und in Partnerarbeit, wobei neben der beruflichen auch die soziale Komponente des Arbeitsalltags einbezogen wird. Grammatik spielt eine untergeordnete Rolle. Erklärungen von Regeln und Übungen sind zwar vorhanden, jedoch auf das Wesentliche begrenzt.

Shopping Matters Band 2 enthält mehrere Wortlisten: eine chronologische, eine alphabetische sowie eine Grundwortschatzliste von ca. 1000 Wörtern, die als bekannt vorausgesetzt werden. Der Anhang enthält darüber hinaus Listen von zusätzlichen Vokabeln für einzelne Branchen, sowie die *Transcripts* für die Hörverstehensübungen und die *Pairwork files* mit den Angaben für die *Information gap*-Übungen bzw. Rollenspiele.

Der Verlag und die Autorin wünschen Ihnen viel Erfolg und Freude bei der Arbeit mit *Shopping Matters*.

Maria Elisabeth Köstler

🎧 Dieses Symbol weist darauf hin, dass sich der Text bzw. Dialog auf der Audio-CD befindet.

Contents

Unit and title	Topics/Language	Grammar	Page
1 On sale	Buying shoes Sales and bargains	If sentences type 1 The passive	*6*
2 Wellness	Fitness and health Parts of the body Sportswear and equipment	The imperative Adverbs and adjectives	*13*
3 Time to spare	Hobbies & sports Buying a bicycle	The infinitive & ing form Expressing the past	*21*
4 A place of my own	Finding a flat In the furniture shop A house-warming party	Have something done 'Make' + verb	*28*
5 Kitchen equipment	Taking a message Spelling Ordering by phone Household gadgets	Modal verbs and substitutes	*37*
6 Electrical appliances and equipment	Household chores How reliable is your household appliance? Operating instructions	If sentences type 2 Comparison of adjectives	*44*
7 Beauty for sale	At the chemist's Animal testing Giving opinions Skincare products	Question tags	*50*

Unit and title	Topics/Language	Grammar	Page
8 *A green world*	A questionnaire Organic food Genetic engineering Agreeing and disagreeing	Prefixes and suffixes	*57*
9 *At a jewellery shop*	Looking for a present Getting a watch repaired Gemstones A burglary	Past progressive and simple past How to express '*lassen*'	*64*
10 *House and home*	At the DIY store Pet equipment and care At the pet shop	The possessive form The apostrophe (')	*71*
11 *Toys and games*	In the toy department The little shoplifter, a short story	Reported speech Words with more than one meaning and homonyms	*77*
12 *Dream job*	Describing your job Job ads A job interview	Simple past and present perfect (continuous) Since/for/ago All/none/both/either/neither	*84*

Appendix

Business correspondence
  Layout, an invoice, a complaint, an e-mail, a website   *91*
Pairwork files   *96*
Transcripts   *101*
Unit word list   *110*
A-Z word list   *123*
Basic word list   *131*
Additional vocabulary   *136*
Common irregular verbs   *141*

UNIT 1 | On sale

🎧 1 Buying shoes

PATRICIA   Hey, Sarah, look at these shoes. They're all in the sale. It says on that sign that they're up to 50 per cent reduced.
SARAH   I like the sandals with the high heels, they're nice.
PATRICIA   Which ones do you mean, the black ones with the flower?
SARAH   No, the ones to the left, the second pair on the right.
PATRICIA   The heels are awfully high. If I wear high heels, I can't walk properly. I like shoes like the ones with the strap.
SARAH   You mean the blue ones at the back? They're boring.
PATRICIA   No, the beige ones on the top shelf, over there on the left.
SARAH   Hm, yes, they're pretty.
PATRICIA   I think they're great and they really are a bargain – only £20. I think I'll go inside and try them on. If they fit, I'll buy them.
SARAH   Well, I can't come with you, I'm afraid. It's very late. If I don't hurry up, I'll miss my bus. But go and buy them now if you like them. Tomorrow they might be gone.

Are the statements true or false? Correct the false statements.

1 All the shoes are reduced in price.
2 Sarah likes the black shoes with the flower.
3 Patricia does not like high heels.
4 Patricia likes the grey shoes on the bottom shelf.
5 The shoes Patricia likes are very expensive.
6 Sarah wants to go to the shoe shop tomorrow.

GRAMMAR CHECK

IF SENTENCES TYPE 1

1. If I **don't** hurry up, I**'ll miss** my bus.
2. If I **wear** high heels, I **can't** walk properly.
3. If you always **look** for special offers, you **save** a lot of money.
4. But **go** and **buy** them now if you **like** them.
5. If the shoes **don't fit** you, **don't buy** them.

- *If-Sätze vom Typ 1: If-Satz mit* simple present – *Hauptsatz mit* will + *Verb* (1).
- *Im Hauptsatz können anstelle von* will *andere Modalverben wie* should *und* can (2), *Verben im* simple present (3) *und in der Befehlsform* (4, 5) *stehen.*

2 Practice

Complete the sentences.

1. If I … (go) now, I … (not/miss) my bus.
2. If I … (not go) now, I … (miss) my bus.
3. I … (give) you a lift if you … (not/catch) your bus.
4. These shoes fit nicely. I … (take) them, if they … (not/be) too expensive.
5. She … (must/ask) for her size if she … (want) to try them on.
6. If we always … (buy) shoes in the sales, we … (save) a lot of money.
7. If these boots … (not/fit), … (try) the next size.
8. If it … (rain) tomorrow, … (not/wear) your new suede shoes.

3 Bargains of the day

Match the if-clauses on the left with the main clauses on the right to make sentences. There are several possible answers.

1. If you come to the Buckle & Heel shoe shop on Monday
2. If you buy two pairs of Cinderella ladies' tights
3. If you buy an Armani handbag or purse
4. If you buy two tins of shoe polish
5. If you send us this coupon
6. If you call this number
7. If you are not satisfied

- you can save 20 cents — 4
- we'll give you your money back — 7
- you can win a prize — 6
- you'll get a free gift — 3
- we'll send you our new catalogue — 5
- you'll get a third pair free — 2
- you'll find a lot of special offers — 1

4 Describing shoes

Use words from the box to describe the shoes.

START LIKE THIS This is a pair of black leather ankle boots with a low heel. These are …

TYPES OF SHOES
court shoe ◆ hiking boot ◆ loafer ◆ oxford shoe
platform soled shoe ◆ slip-on shoe ◆ sling back shoe
strappy shoe ◆ mule ◆ ankle boot ◆ lace-up shoe
knee-high boot ◆ trainers ◆ sandals

MATERIAL
leather upper ◆ coated leather ◆ suede ◆ nubuck ◆ waxy leather
patent leather ◆ synthetic material ◆ fabric ◆ canvas

OTHER USEFUL WORDS
buckle ◆ laces ◆ high-heeled / with a high heel ◆ with a medium heel
low-heeled / with a low heel ◆ stiletto heel ◆ wedge heel ◆ open toe
waterproof ◆ wide fitting ◆ cleated sole ◆ rubber sole
hard-wearing ◆ padded ankle collar ◆ padded insole
padded tongue ◆ leather lining ◆ toe cap

5 What are you wearing?

With a partner, take it in turns to describe the shoes you are wearing today. What other kinds of shoes do you have at home?

6 In the shoe shop

Listen to the dialogue and answer the questions.

1 What does Patricia ask for?
2 What size does she need?
3 Which sizes are the shoes available in?
4 Why don't they fit?
5 What does the shop assistant suggest?
6 When does Patricia want to go to the branch in Orchard street?
7 When do they close?
8 What is the time now?
9 What does the shop assistant want to do before Patricia goes to the other shop?

7 Practice

Complete the sentences using the words below.

> another ◆ get ◆ hurts ◆ just ◆ left ◆ on ◆ past ◆ plenty ◆ right ◆ take ◆ tight ◆ top ◆ up

1 I'd like to try … the shoes with the buckle. *on*
2 The grey ones on the … shelf. *top*
3 Just a moment, I'll … them. *get*
4 Please, … a seat. *take*
5 I've only got size six … *left*
6 They are too … at the toes. *tight*
7 When I walk around, it … . *hurts*
8 We've got … branch in Orchard Street. *another*
9 I can go there … now. *right*
10 It's only a quarter … six now, there's … of time. *past / plenty*
11 If you … wait a minute, I'll ring them … . *just / up*

UNIT 1 | 9

8 Which shoes are where?

Use the words below to describe where the shoes are in the picture. Look at the example first.

> in front of ◆ behind ◆ below ◆ on top of ◆ under ◆ between
> to the left of ◆ on ◆ next to ◆ on the bottom ◆ in the middle of

EXAMPLE 0 … the bed   *The black oxfords are under the bed.*

1 on the rug
2 … the window below
3 … the cat behind
4 … the books between
5 … the trainers to the left of
6 … the plant next to
7 … shelf on the bottom
8 … the television on top of
9 … the television in front of
10 … the room in the middle of

GRAMMAR CHECK

THE PASSIVE

1 Most shoes **are made** of leather.
2 Many articles **will be sold** at half price.
3 The price **was reduced**.
4 This shoe polish **must not be used** on suede leather.
5 This handbag **was designed by** Giorgio Armani.

- *Das Passiv wird mit einer Form von* be + *Partizip Perfekt gebildet (1–3).*
- *Das Passiv mit Modalverben (can, must usw.) wird mit Modalverb +* be + *Partizip Perfekt gebildet (4).*
- *Das Passiv wird verwendet, um Handlungen zu beschreiben, ohne deren Urheber nennen zu müssen (z. B. in Gebrauchsanweisungen). Möchte man den Urheber nennen, verwendet man* by *(5).*

9 Sale of the season

Use the words in the brackets to form passive sentences.

1 Lots of bargains … (can/find) at Brown's department store.
2 Many prices … (reduce).
3 The prices for shoes and leatherware … (cut) by up to 50 per cent.
4 Hundreds of toys and games … (sell) for under £5.
5 Skis and bindings … (can/buy) at half price.
6 In our TV and video department many items … (sell) at up to 30 per cent off.

brown's

10 Practice

Use the words in the brackets to form passive sentences.

1 This shoe polish … (can/use) on most leather shoes.
2 Shoe polish … (must not/use) on suede.
3 All suede shoes … (should/impregnate) with a water-proofing spray.
4 These black patent leather shoes … (make) in Italy.
5 These classic court shoes … (can/wear) on most occasions.
6 Next Monday the new shop … (open).
7 Last week 120 pairs of trainers … (sell) in this shop.

SHOES

European size	36–37	38	39–40	40–41	42	43	44
British size	4	5	6	7	8	9	10
USA	$5\frac{1}{2}$	$6\frac{1}{2}$	$7\frac{1}{2}$	$8\frac{1}{2}$	$9\frac{1}{2}$	$10\frac{1}{2}$	$11\frac{1}{2}$

11 A sales dialogue

Work with a partner to make a dialogue in English.

Customer

Sagen Sie, dass Sie im Schaufenster Schuhe gesehen haben, die Ihnen gefallen.

Sagen Sie, wo die Schuhe sind.

Sagen Sie, dass Sie nur die englische Größe wissen, aber nicht die deutsche. Sagen Sie die Größe (z. B. 6).

Sagen Sie, welche Sie probieren möchten.

Sagen Sie, dass die Größe passt, dass Sie aber noch ein anderes Paar probieren möchten.

Fragen Sie nach dem Preis.

Sagen Sie, dass Sie die Schuhe nehmen werden.

Sagen Sie, dass Sie keine Schuhcreme brauchen.

Sagen Sie wie Sie zahlen möchten.

Shop assistant

Fragen Sie, welche.

Fragen Sie nach der Größe.

Sagen Sie, welcher deutschen Größe das entspricht. Sagen Sie, dass Sie die Schuhe holen werden und bitten Sie ihn/sie, Platz zu nehmen.
    Zeigen Sie das gewünschte Paar und zwei ähnliche Paare in derselben Größe.

Fragen Sie, ob die Größe passt.

Sagen Sie, dass die Schuhe die neueste Mode aus Italien sind.

Sagen Sie den Preis und sagen Sie, dass die Schuhe jetzt besonders günstig sind, eine gute Qualität haben und aus echtem Leder sind.

Bieten Sie Schuhcreme in der selben Farbe an.

Fragen Sie, wie er/sie zahlen möchte.

UNIT 2 | Wellness

1 | Test yourself

Read the following questions and decide which of the answers most applies to you.

9 Questions on your Fitness and Health

1 How often do you exercise (30 minutes at least)?
a ~~less than once a week~~ o
b once or twice a week
c 3 times a week or more

2 Do you use the stairs instead of the lift or escalator?
a never
~~b~~ sometimes
c always

3 Are you overweight or underweight?
a by more than 10 per cent
~~b~~ by a little
c not at all

4 How many cigarettes do you smoke?
a more than 10 a day
b up to 10 a day
~~c~~ none at all

5 Do you drink alcohol?
a regularly (4 or more glasses of wine – or equivalent – a week)
b sometimes (about 2 or 3 glasses a week)
~~c~~ never or very little (not more than 1 glass a week)

6 Do you eat fried food like chips, sausages or hamburgers?
a nearly every day
b 2 to 4 times a week
~~c~~ once a week or less

7 Do you eat a lot of processed food like white bread, cakes, chocolate etc?
a nearly every day
b 2 to 4 times a week
~~c~~ once a week or less

8 Do you eat fruit and vegetables?
a hardly ever
b 2 or 3 times a week
~~c~~ every day

9 You've got a day off and the sun is shining. What do you do?
a I stay at home and watch TV.
b I go to the nearest park and lie in the sun.
~~c~~ I enjoy an outdoor activity like cycling or in-line skating.

And here are your scores.

You get 0 points for every a, 1 point for every b and 2 points for every c answer.

13–18 Congratulations. You seem to be in good shape and know everything about the advantages of a well balanced diet. You know that people who feel good often also look good. But be careful not to overdo it. Fitness isn't everything and too much exercise can even be bad for you. It's also important to develop the social and intellectual sides of your life by having hobbies and spending time with friends.

7–12 Not too bad. You know what is good for you and what isn't, but you don't always find it easy to do the right thing. There is a lot of healthy food that tastes good – eat that instead of too much junk food. Planning your meals in advance can help. Try to find some activities you enjoy and soon you'll see that you can cope better with stress, you'll relax and feel less tense – and you might even make some new friends too.

0–6 You really don't care very much about your needs. If you don't look after yourself a bit more, you'll soon have serious health problems. Did you know that regular exercise reduces depression and anxiety and leads to more productivity at work? Start with 5 or 10 minutes exercise every day and increase it gradually. Maybe you can also find a way to a more healthy diet.

2 Working with words

Match the German words on the left with their English translations on the right.

1	angespannt	anxiety	12
2	bewältigen, schaffen	cope	2
3	denaturierte Lebensmittel	diet	4
4	Ernährung	enjoy	7
5	ernsthaft	exercise	13
6	Form	gradually	14
7	genießen	health	8
8	Gesundheit	in advance	9
9	im Voraus	junk food	10
10	minderwertiges Essen	overdo	15
11	sich erholen, entspannen	processed food	3
12	Sorge, Angst	relax	11
13	sportliche Betätigung	serious	5
14	stufenweise	shape	6
15	übertreiben	tense	1

3 Opposites

Unscramble the words on the right to find the opposites of the words on the left. Then translate both into German.

1. overweight ECDASERE 4
2. healthy ERUEINHDWGT 1
3. regular AUDBLNNCEA 6
4. increase ELATNHUYH 2
5. advantage EIURGLRRA 3
6. balanced VDIADNAATEGS 5

> **GRAMMAR CHECK**
>
> **THE IMPERATIVE**
>
> 1. **Start** with 5 minutes a day … and **increase** it gradually.
> 2. **Be** careful, you two!
> 3. **Don't drink** a lot of alcohol.
> 4. **Never forget** to drink plenty of fluids.
>
> - *Man verwendet den Imperativ für Hinweise, Befehle, Warnungen, und Erklärungen. Der Imperativ ist die Grundform des Verbs (1, 2).*
> - *Man verwendet dieselbe Form, wenn man zu einer oder mehreren Personen spricht (2, 3). Beachten Sie, dass es im Englischen keine Unterscheidung zwischen ‚du' und ‚Sie' gibt.*
> - *Negative Formen werden mit* don't *gebildet (3). Bei negativen Formen mit* never *entfällt* don't *(4).*

4 Practice

Look at the following icons and write sentences using the imperative.

EXAMPLE Don't always take the lift or escalator.
Use the stairs more often.

5 Parts of the body

Find words in the puzzle to label the drawing above. You may use a dictionary for help.

B	A	C	K	I	Z	T	D	F	I	E	A
B	O	T	T	O	M	P	S	N	V	O	R
M	Q	F	I	N	G	E	R	J	A	T	M
H	G	U	O	L	G	N	S	S	O	H	P
S	T	O	M	A	C	H	P	P	V	S	R
J	F	A	C	E	H	I	N	T	I	H	E
C	A	L	F	E	N	E	K	E	X	H	D
T	Q	L	A	E	C	Q	N	E	S	L	L
H	O	D	T	K	D	M	E	S	Q	E	U
I	W	A	I	S	T	S	E	H	C	G	O
G	E	L	B	O	W	P	A	L	O	W	H
H	T	O	O	F	T	S	I	R	W	G	S

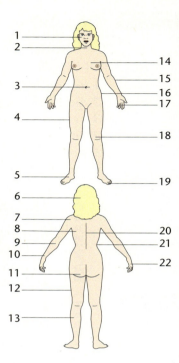

6 Think more clearly

Complete the text using the words in the box, then listen to the CD and check your answers.

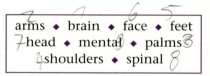

arms ◆ brain ◆ face ◆ feet
head ◆ mental ◆ palms
shoulders ◆ spinal

Boost blood flow to the …¹ with this easy yoga move.

How to do it

Stand erect with …² outstretched, …³ down. Arms should be in line with …⁴. Picture a clock on the floor, under your …⁵, …⁶ up. Then begin to spin, turning in a clockwise direction. Begin and end slowly, building up speed and slowing down gradually. Focus your vision on a single point ahead of you to prevent yourself from getting too dizzy.

How it works

Spinning enhances circulation, which in turn increases the energy flow through the top of the …⁷. It also aids the flow of …⁸ fluid, which contributes to …⁹ clarity.

GRAMMAR CHECK

ADJECTIVES AND ADVERBS

1 Begin and end **slowly** … and slowing down **gradually**.
2 You might become **seriously** ill.
3 You'll soon have **serious** health problems.
4 Be **careful** not to overdo it.
5 People who feel **good** often also look **good**.

- *Ein Adverb beschreibt eine Handlung und bezieht sich oft auf ein Verb (1) oder Adjektiv (2).*
- *Ein Adjektiv beschreibt einen Zustand und bezieht sich auf ein Hauptwort oder eine Person (3, 4).*
- *Ein Adjektiv steht nach* be *(4) sowie den Verben* look *(aussehen),* feel *(fühlen) (5),* smell *(riechen),* taste *(schmecken),* sound *(klingen),* seem *(scheinen)* become *(werden) und* get *(werden).*

7 Practice

Choose the correct word to complete each sentence.

1 He is very *serious/seriously* about learning tennis.
2 You can *easy/easily* run that far.
3 She is *serious/seriously* interested in learning a new sport.
4 This fruit juice tastes *good/well*.
5 It seems quite *easy/easily* to me.
6 That idea sounds *terrible/terribly*.
7 He's ill! That's *terrible/terribly* news.
8 He is in *bad/badly* shape.
9 That drink tastes very *bitter/bitterly*.
10 That exercise is very *good/well*.
11 They have done very *bad/badly* with their exercises.
12 The cycling trip was *good/well* organized.

UNIT 2

8 A radio talk show

Look at this excerpt from a radio talk show and fill in the gaps with adverbs or adjectives. Listen to the CD to check your answers.

DJ Dr Runner, can you tell our listeners why it is so important to do …1 (regular) exercise?

RUNNER If you are …2 (physical) inactive, you may have a higher risk of coronary heart disease. But …3 (physical) inactivity is just one of many risk factors involved. These factors also include diabetes, cigarette smoking, high cholesterol and extreme overweight. …4 (regular) exercise strengthens your heart and lungs and makes them work better. When you exercise …5 (regular), you burn calories. Exercise also builds and strengthens bones, joints and muscles. It prevents …6 (high) blood pressure and lowers the cholesterol level.

DJ Are there any risks involved in exercising?

RUNNER Well, if done …7 (proper) and …8 (sensible), exercise should be a …9 (safe) and …10 (pleasant) experience. You should consult a doctor if you have chest pain, joint or bone problems or if you become breathless …11 (easy).

DJ Which exercises should I do?

RUNNER Pick activities you enjoy. You are more likely to stay with your exercise programme if you do something you like. Very …12 (good) for your heart and lungs, for example, are the following activities: brisk walking, aerobics, dancing, cycling, cross-country skiing, skating, jogging, swimming and tennis.

DJ Do I need to be …13 (special) equipped or dressed to exercise?

RUNNER As you can see from the suggested list of sports and exercises, many activities do not require …14 (special) equipment or clothing. You should dress …15 (appropriate) for the activity and weather. Choose …16 (loose)-fitting, …17 (comfortable) clothes and shoes. Do not use rubberized, nonporous material.

DJ One last piece of advice you would like to give us?

RUNNER Remember to drink lots of fluids before, during and after exercise.

DJ That was …18 (high) interesting. Thank you very much for the interview, Doctor Runner. And now let's take some callers.

9 Questions and answers

After the interview, people call in with questions for Dr Runner. Listen to or read the interview again and answer their questions.

1 "I feel fine but my doctor says I should exercise. Why?"
2 "I go jogging a lot and sometimes I have chest pain. Is this normal?"
3 "What does regular exercise do to your heart and lungs?"
4 "There are so many types of sports and activities. How do I decide which is right for me?"
5 "I hate fitness centres. What kind of outdoor activities are good for my heart?"
6 "I'd like to start cycling. Do I need any special clothing? Is it a good idea to carry a water bottle with me?"

10 Getting equipped

Look at the illustrations and find the matching descriptions. Which outfit would you prefer to wear? Why?

Hooded sweat cardigan with two front pockets, long sleeves and a drawcord fastening. Washable. Cotton. Grey, black or green. Men's sizes S, M, L, XL. **€75.00**

Tracksuit bottoms with elasticated drawcord waist and tape detail down the side of the leg. Washable. Polyester. Brown. **€22.00** YX 1381 S, M, L, XL **€34.00**

Cotton jersey leggings. Lycra for a perfect fit. Ankle length. Washable. 80% cotton, 15% polyester, 5% Lycra. Navy, black or grey.
Short fitting sizes (inside leg 27 ins) S, M, L, XL **€18.50**.
Standard fitting sizes (inside leg 29 ins) S, M, L, XL **€19.50**.

Tank top. Washable. 95% cotton, 5% Lycra. Blue, chocolate or red. Sizes S, M, L, XL **€10.50**

Fleece top with two side pockets and embroidered logo. Polyester polar fleece. Lilac, cherry or lemon. Sizes S, M, L, XL **€68.00**

Tracksuit. Top with front zip fastening and two side pockets. Bottoms with elasticated waist. Tape detail. 100% polyester. Lilac, green. Sizes S, M, L, XL **€53.50**

11 In a sports shop

Unscramble the dialogue and read it with a partner.

Customer

- *11* All right, I'll take that.
- *9* How much is the whole set?
- *13* No thank you, that's all. Where can I pay?
- *3* He'll need a medium. These shorts here look nice. What material are they?
- *5* Yes, they look nice.
- *7* No, I like that navy. Have you got a matching football shirt?
- *1* I'm looking for football shorts and a shirt for my son.

Shop assistant

- *6* They are also available in other colours if you like.
- *12* Is there anything else I can do for you?
- *14* The cash desk is over there.
- *8* What about this one here? It's also polyester and we've also got it in different colours.
- *10* That's €15 for the shorts and €30 for the shirt, that's €45 all together.
- *4* They are 100% polyester, and they are of course machine washable. They have an elasticated waist and embroidered logo here on the left leg.
- *2* Would you like to have a look? All our football equipment is over here. What size does your son take?

12 Buying sportswear

In pairs, practise buying the sportswear in Exercise 10. Student A: you are the shop assistant. Look at File 1 on page 96. Student B: you want to buy the items below. Find out if they're still available and ask questions about the material and care instructions.

START LIKE THIS Hello, I'm looking for the tank tops that were advertised yesterday in the paper. …

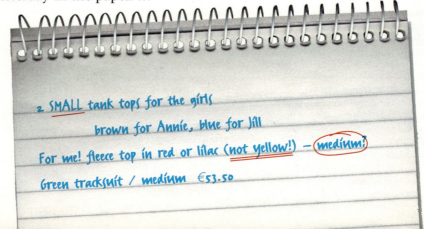

2 SMALL tank tops for the girls
brown for Annie, blue for Jill
For me! fleece top in red or lilac (not yellow!) — (medium!)
Green tracksuit / medium €53.50

UNIT 3 | Time to spare

1 Spare time activities

Look at the pictures. Which spare time activities can you identify?

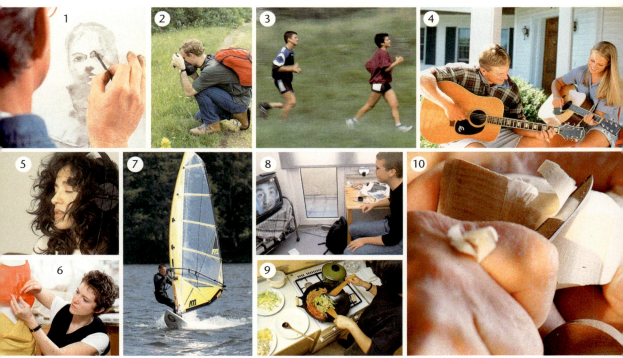

cooking ◆ jogging ◆ listening to music ◆ painting
playing the guitar ◆ sewing ◆ taking photos ◆ watching TV
windsurfing ◆ doing woodwork

2 What's your hobby?

Listen to five people talk about their hobbies and take notes. Then answer the following questions.

1 Who likes doing sport? Pamella
2 Who prefers playing on a team? Denis
3 Who is interested in designing clothes? Josmina
4 Who loves doing outdoor activities? Bryan
5 Who would like to live in a foreign country? Kim

GRAMMAR CHECK

THE INFINITIVE AND THE ING FORM AFTER A VERB

1 We **failed to reach** the semi-finals.
2 She **enjoys skiing** very much.
3 I really **hate cooking**. / I really **hate to cook**.

- Einige Verben stehen mit dem to-*Infinitiv* (1), andere mit der ing-*Form* (2). Bei manchen Verben sind beide Formen möglich (3).

Beachten Sie folgende Listen:

to-Infinitiv	ing-Form	beide Formen
can afford to	be good at …-ing	hate to … / hate …-ing
fail to	be interested in …-ing	like to … / like …-ing
hope to	be keen on …-ing	love to… / love -ing
learn to	enjoy …-ing	start to … / start …-ing
plan to	look forward to …-ing	
refuse to	practise …-ing	
try to	prefer …-ing	
would like to	succeed in …-ing	

3 Practice

Complete the sentences with the right verb form.

1 I like … (travel) a lot and I'd love … (go) to Hawaii one day, but I'm afraid I can't afford … (go) there now.
2 I'm quite good at … (paint) and … (draw) and I'm planning … (attend) a course.
3 I started … (work) with textiles at school but I'm not keen on … (sew).
4 I love … (ski) and I am looking forward to … (spend) my next winter holidays in the Alps.
5 My parents love … (go) to operas but I am not interested in … (listen) to classical music so I usually refuse … (go) with them.
6 I'm learning … (play) tennis so I practise … (play) nearly every day.
7 I have often tried … (come) first but I have never succeeded in … (win) a race.

4 What about you?

In turns, talk about the things you like and don't like to do in your spare time. Use the words from the three lists in the grammar check.

5 Tennis – first steps

Right from the start

Get your technique correct from the start. Begin by having a one-to-one lesson from a professional – it'll make a world of difference. Buy a mid-sized, lightweight racket. These are usually made of graphite. Choose your tennis shoes according to the court you will be playing on. Indoor courts require shoes with no tread; outdoor courts require a good tread. Some clubs ask for tennis whites – check first. Try to have one lesson a week. Join a group of friends and play as much as possible between lessons, remembering to practise everything you've been taught. Don't play too hard to begin with as this will give you less chance of hitting the ball into the right area of the court. The ultimate challenge: Join a local team and play in tournaments.

Read the text above and find the English translations of the following German words. Then translate the whole text.

1 Technik
2 Einzelunterricht
3 riesiger Unterschied
4 mittelgroß
5 üblicherweise
6 ensprechend
7 (Tennis-)Platz
8 erfordern
9 Profil
10 beigebracht
11 schlagen, treffen
12 Bereich
13 allerletzte/r/s, allergrößte/r/s
14 Herausforderung
15 beitreten, Mitglied werden
16 Turnier, Wettkampf

UNIT 3

6 Buying a bicycle

CUSTOMER	Excuse me.
ASSISTANT	Yes? How can I help you?
CUSTOMER	I'm looking for a bicycle.
ASSISTANT	What kind of bicycle are you looking for, sir?
CUSTOMER	I don't really know. The prices vary a lot. What are the differences between all these bikes here?
ASSISTANT	Well, you see, the more expensive they are, the better the material. This one here for example is very lightweight but strong at the same time. And it has got 21 speeds. It's the best bicycle we've got.
CUSTOMER	But it costs an awful lot.
ASSISTANT	Well, it is expensive but if you're a passionate biker, it's worth the price. Where and how often do you plan to ride it?
CUSTOMER	I'd like to use the bike for going to work, here in town, and to make short trips in the surrounding areas. But we haven't really got any high mountains around here, so I don't think I'd need 21 speeds. I used to have a bike, you know. It rode beautifully, although it was quite old. But someone stole it last year.
ASSISTANT	What a pity. Bicycle theft has become quite a problem lately. Was the bike locked?
CUSTOMER	Yes, I had locked it properly but it was stolen anyway. I always used to lock it with a chain and combination lock, but that was not very secure, I'm afraid.
ASSISTANT	No, a shackle lock is much better, much more secure.
CUSTOMER	Well, if I get a new bike, I'll buy a proper lock too. You know, I haven't ridden a bike since mine was stolen, and I really miss it.
ASSISTANT	Now, what about this bicycle here? It combines traditional styling with the best modern technology. It's got shimano 7-speed gears, 26-inch wheels and it has also got mudguards and a prop stand. We could also attach a luggage carrier if you want.
CUSTOMER	Yes, that'd be good since I'd like to use the bike for shopping too. How much is this model?

ASSISTANT	It's on special offer now, it was €369 and now it's only €269.
CUSTOMER	May I have a try?
ASSISTANT	Certainly. You can go outside to the car park if you like. But I'll need some ID if you want to leave the shop.
CUSTOMER	OK, here's my driving licence.

Answer the questions.

1 What is the difference between the cheaper and the more expensive bicycles?
2 Where does the customer want to ride his bike?
3 What happened to his old bike?
4 What kind of lock does the shop assistant suggest?
5 What are the features of the bike the shop assistant offers?
6 Why would the customer like a luggage carrier?
7 How much does the bicycle cost now?
8 Where can the customer try it out?

7 Bicycles

Can you find the translations of the English words?

Bügelschloss ◆ Fahrradständer ◆ Felge ◆ Gabel ◆ Gangschaltung ◆ Gepäckträger ◆ Glocke ◆ Lenker ◆ Hinterradbremsen ◆ Kette ◆ Kettenschutz ◆ Schutzblech ◆ Pedal ◆ Pumpe ◆ Rad ◆ Rahmen ◆ Reifen ◆ Rückstrahler ◆ Sattel ◆ Scheinwerfer, Lampe ◆ Schlauch ◆ Vorderradbremsen

GRAMMAR CHECK

EXPRESSING THE PAST

1 I **used to have** a bike.
2 **Did** you **use to ride** much when you were a child?
3 It **rode** wonderfully, although it **was** quite old.
4 But someone **stole** it last year.
5 I **had locked** the bike properly but it was stolen anyway.
6 I **haven't ridden** a bike **since** mine was stolen.
7 Bicycle theft **has become** quite a problem **lately**.

- Used to *bezieht sich auf gewohnheitsmäßige Handlungen in der Vergangenheit oder auf einen Zustand in der Vergangenheit (1, 2).*
- *Das* simple past *wird verwendet, um in der Vergangenheit bereits abgeschlossene Handlungen zu schildern oder Zustände zu beschreiben. Der Zeitpunkt der Handlung ist entweder bekannt (3) oder wird genannt (4).*
- *Das* past perfect *wird verwendet, um auszudrücken, dass eine Handlung oder ein Zustand in der Vergangenheit bereits abgeschlossen war, als etwas Neues geschah (5).*
- *Um zu verdeutlichen, dass eine Handlung oder ein Zustand in der Vergangenheit begonnen hat und noch andauert, wird das* present perfect *verwendet, häufig in Verbindung mit* since *oder* for *(6). Das* present perfect *wird oft in Verwendung mit Adverbien wie* already, never, lately *(7) usw. benutzt.* *just, already, ever, never, yet/not yet, since, for, lately, up to now, so far, how long*

8 Practice

Complete the sentences with *used to* and the correct form of the verb.

EXAMPLES   Where ... (live) when you were a child? *Where did you use to live when you were a child?*
We ... (live) in a small village. *We used to live in a small village.*

1 What ... (do) in your summer holidays?
2 My parents and I ... (not spend) our holidays at the seaside.
3 We ... (stay) at home most of the time.
4 She ... (be) married but now she is divorced.
5 He ... (speak) German quite well but I'm afraid he has forgotten most of it.
6 We ... (be) neighbours but then they moved away.
7 Brian ... (not go) to work by car, but now he does.
8 We ... (work) in the same shop but now she is unemployed.

9 Practice

Combine the two sentences into one sentence. Use the word in brackets and the past perfect in either the first or the second part of the sentence.

EXAMPLE The goods arrived. We informed the customer that they were here. (after)
After the goods had arrived we informed the customer that they were here.

1 He did not leave the house. We told him to go. (until)
2 The teacher corrected our tests. She said they were good. (when)
3 She locked the door of her shop. She went home. (after)
4 He did not want to buy the couch. His wife saw it. (before)
5 We reduced the price. We finally sold the bike. (after)
6 She did not pay the bill. I sent her two reminders. (before)

10 Practice

Rewrite the sentences with the simple past or present perfect form of the verbs.

1 I ... (buy) my bike 10 years ago.
2 Someone ... (steal) it last year.
3 Since then I ... (not/have) a bike.
4 My friend ... (go) to Paris last year.
5 I ... (never/be) to France.
6 I think I ... (already/see) him today.
7 I ... (go) to the Tyrol last winter.
8 ... (you/ever/try) to ski?
9 She ... (work) for this company for several years now.
10 She ... (start) to work for them 5 years ago.
11 We ... (move) into this house when I was three.
12 We ... (live) in this house since I was three.

11 What about you?

Write down three of your favourite spare time activities. Make a list of things you need for it. Then walk around the class and find someone who likes the same things. Together make up a sales dialogue for buying the equipment.

WELL, I LIKE TO SWIM. ALL I NEED FOR THAT IS A SWIMMING COSTUME AND PERHAPS A PAIR OF GOGGLES

UNIT 4 | A place of my own

1 Patricia's new home

Patricia Taylor is looking for a place of her own. Rents are very high so she hopes to find a flat she can share with other people.

Listen to the telephone conversation and find out which ad the people are talking about.

TURNPIKE LANE
Third person to share house, 1 large room, share k&b, £70 pw + dep
☎ 0208 738615

WIMBLEDON
Fem for sgle rm 1st flr, CH, flat with gdn £95 pw
☎ 0208 446904

CLAPHAM nr tube
Own rm in house, share lounge, CH, w/machine, t/dryer, £100 pw + deposit
☎ 0207 864333

2 Abbreviations

What do the abbreviations stand for?

1 k&b
2 fem
3 CH
4 pw
5 rm
6 dep
7 nr
8 w/machine
9 gdn
10 sgle
11 t/dryer

3 What's the place like?

Listen again to the CD. Which of the following words describe the house? What do you know about the other people who live there?

five bedrooms ◆ free lunch ◆ lounge ◆ detached house
semi-detached house ◆ kitchen ◆ bathroom ◆ balcony ◆ garden
gas central heating ◆ dishwasher ◆ lift ◆ washing machine
tumble-dryer ◆ hair-dryer

4 Patricia's new home

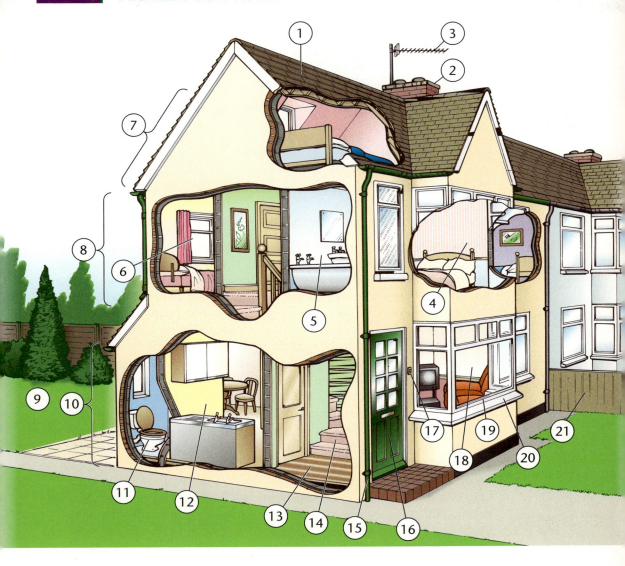

What parts of the house can you identify?

9 back garden • 5 bathroom • 19 bay window • 4 bedroom • 2 chimney
17 doorbell • 15 drainpipe • 21 fence • 8 first floor • 16 front door
10 ground floor • 13 hall • 12 kitchen • 18 lounge • 1 roof • 14 stairs
7 top floor • 3 TV aerial • 11 WC • 6 window • 20 window sill

UNIT 4 | 29

5 Moving in

Patricia calls her friend Sarah to tell her about her new room.

"It's on the first floor and faces the garden, so I think it will be very quiet. ... The garden? Yes, it's very nice, it will be great for parties. The landlady says that she has the garden looked after – you know, she has the grass cut regularly and things like that – so it always looks very nice. ... Oh yes, there's lots to do, like paint, put up wallpaper and lay down a new carpet. ... Well, my father and I will probably do the painting ourselves but I'll have to have the carpet fitted. My father says we can't do that ourselves. ... No, it's unfurnished, there's no furniture at all. I'm going to take some furniture from my old room – the wardrobe, the desk and some bookshelves. We're getting it transported – the pieces are too heavy for us to move ourselves. ... No, I won't keep my old bed. I think I'll buy a sofa that can be turned into a bed, you know, a sofa bed. I know it's a bit complicated to do that every night, but I'd like to have a sofa and there isn't enough room for both. ... Well, there's not a lot of light but it's certainly not too dark. There's a big window with some ugly curtains. The landlady had them made about 10 years ago. She says they're still good as new, but I'm going to put up new ones. Do you think I can sew them myself? Perhaps I should get them made – I'm not very good at sewing."

Are the sentences true or false? Correct the false sentences.

1 Patricia's new room faces the street.
2 The landlady looks after the garden herself.
3 Patricia wants to have the walls painted.
4 Patricia's father will help her to paint the room.
5 Someone is going to lay the carpet for her.
6 She's going to take the bed and the desk from her old room.
7 She and her parents are going to move the furniture themselves.
8 She wants to buy a sofa.
9 She is afraid that the room is too dark.
10 She wants to use the curtains that are already in the room.

GRAMMAR CHECK

HAVE SOMETHING DONE

1. She **has the grass cut** regularly.
2. She **doesn't have it cut** every week.
3. I'll have to **have the carpet fitted**.
4. The landlady **had them made** about 10 years ago.
5. Perhaps I should **get the curtains made**.

- *Das Satzmuster* have + Objekt + past participle *wird im Sinne von ‚etwas machen lassen' gebraucht (1–4). Fragen und Verneinungen werden mit einer Form von* do *gebildet (2).*
- *Anstatt* have *kann man auch* get *verwenden (4).* Get *ist etwas informeller als* have.

⚠ *Dieses Satzmuster nicht mit dem* present perfect *verwechseln.*
She has the grass cut. *Sie lässt das Gras mähen.*

She has cut the grass.
(present perfect)
Sie hat das Gras gemäht.

6 Practice

Rearrange the words in brackets to complete the sentences.

EXAMPLE This suit doesn't fit properly. (altered I'd to have like it).
This suit doesn't fit properly. I'd like to have it altered.

1. Sally went to the hairdresser's last week, (her hair dyed she had).
2. (her cut had Sheila hair), she looks quite different now.
3. The jeans are too long. (shortened have can them we?)
4. The washing machine doesn't work anymore so (have repaired we it must).
5. She can't lay the carpet herself, (have must she done it).
6. Our car is not big enough for that sofa, (must delivered have it we).
7. The tap is dripping, (it should get we fixed straight away).
8. Their central heating wasn't working any more, so (installed got a they new one).

7 In the furniture shop

Patricia and her mother go to a furniture shop to pick out a sofa.

PATRICIA	I like this sofa bed here very much, but I'm not sure about the colour.
SHOP ASSISTANT	What colours have you got in your living room?
PATRICIA	I've got a blue carpet and the wallpaper is cream with stripes. I haven't bought any curtains yet, I've only just moved in, you know.
SHOP ASSISTANT	Well, any of these shades would be fine, perhaps not the dark blue one, though. It might clash with the colour of the carpet.
PATRICIA	Actually, I would prefer a lighter shade because the room isn't very big and dark colours would make it look even smaller. What do you think, mum?
MOTHER	I'm not so sure, a very light colour will soon look dirty.
SHOP ASSISTANT	So you should have something that's easy to clean. Have you seen this sofa over here? It's got loose covers and, look, the zip fastening makes them easy to remove.
MOTHER	That sounds interesting. Can they be washed?
SHOP ASSISTANT	Yes, you can wash them at 40°C and you can spin-dry them, but you mustn't tumble-dry them. And they are non-iron.
MOTHER	But 40°C is not very hot, they won't get clean at that temperature.
SHOP ASSISTANT	I think they will. If you've got really nasty stains you could use a special detergent.
PATRICIA	Hm, I'm not so sure.
SHOP ASSISTANT	And what about leather? Most of these sofas here are available in leather as well.

PATRICIA   Isn't leather a very difficult material to care for?
SHOP ASSISTANT   No, not at all. Suede needs careful treatment but this soft nappa leather here is very durable.
PATRICIA   But leather is very expensive, isn't it?
SHOP ASSISTANT   It only costs a bit more than fabric does but it'll keep much longer.

Answer the questions.
1 What are the main colours in Patricia's room?
2 Why does Patricia want a light colour?
3 What is Patricia's mother worried about?
4 Why does the shop assistant recommend leather?

> **MAKE + VERB**
>
> I make you smile. *Ich bringe dich zum Lächeln.*
> She made me buy that sofa. *Sie brachte mich dazu, das Sofa zu kaufen.*
> It makes her look older. *Es lässt sie älter aussehen.*

8 Practice

Find the matching pairs of sentences and translate them.

1 Grey doesn't suit me.   But he made her go on.
2 Jeremy is a very funny man.   Dark colours will make it look even smaller.
3 We shouldn't take the pale blue sofa.   He makes everybody laugh.
4 The new haircut suits you.   It made everybody cry.
5 The room is small already.   It makes me look so pale.
6 She wanted to give up.   It makes you look much younger.
7 I'm completely exhausted.   The children will soon make it look dirty.
8 The ending of the film was so sad.   The gym teacher made us run all afternoon.

9 What's where?

Work in pairs. Student A should look at the plan of Patricia's room on this page. Student B should look at the plan in File 10 on page 100. Take turns to describe to each other where things are in the room, and try to find as many differences between the two plans as possible.

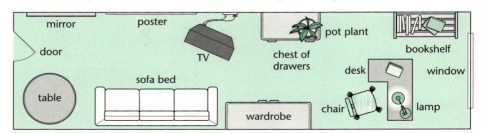

10 A sales dialogue

Look at the extracts from the catalogue and use the flow chart to act out a sales dialogue.

READY-MADE SATIN CURTAINS, available with the latest tab-top look or 7.5 cm heading tape. Valances, tie-backs and cushion covers available separately. Material: 50 % polyester, 50 % cotton.
1. Breton design: blue, green or yellow
2. Hessian design: green, yellow or ocean-blue.

Curtains – 7.5 cm heading tape
Pair fits rail width up to 160 cm.
Single curtain width 125 cm.

1 Breton	2 Hessian	Drop (cm)	Price (pair)
BY 5634	HX 7539	120	£15.00
BY 5644	HX 7549	135	£20.00
BY 5654	HX 7559	180	£30.00
BY 5664	HX 7569	225	£35.00

Curtains – tab-top
Pair fits rail width up to 160 cm.
Single curtain width 125 cm.

1 Breton	2 Hessian	Drop (cm)	Price (pair)
BY 1234	HX 6455	120	£24.00
BY 1244	HX 6465	135	£29.00
BY 1254	HX 6475	180	£35.00
BY 1264	HX 6485	225	£42.00

Customer

Sagen Sie, dass Sie einen Fertigvorhang kaufen möchten.

Sagen Sie, dass Ihr Fenster 125 cm breit ist.

Sagen Sie, was Sie lieber möchten. Sagen Sie, dass Ihnen das Muster von Breton gut gefällt, aber die Farbe etwas zu dunkel ist.

Fragen Sie, wie viel der gelbe Vorhang kostet und wie lange eine Bestellung dauern würde.

Sagen Sie, wie lang der Vorhang sein soll.

Fragen Sie, welches Material der Vorhang ist.

Sagen Sie, welchen Vorhang Sie bestellen möchten.

Shop assistant

Fragen Sie nach der Größe des Fensters.

Zeigen Sie den Kunden verschiedene Fertigvorhänge, und sagen Sie dass, es die meisten mit Schlaufen oder Vorhangbändern gibt.

Sagen Sie, dass es den Vorhang auch in grün und gelb gibt und zeigen Sie ein Muster (sample). Der gelbe ist aber im Moment nicht auf Lager.

Sagen Sie, eine Bestellung würde etwa eine Woche dauern. Fragen Sie nach der Länge des Vorhanges.

Sagen Sie den Preis.

Sagen Sie das Material.

Sagen Sie, dass Sie ein Bestellformular holen.

11 Buy the best sofa ever!

In groups of three or four, write down the words you don't understand and look them up in a dictionary. Then translate the text. When you have finished compare your translation with the other groups.

Master the art

Buy the best sofa ever!

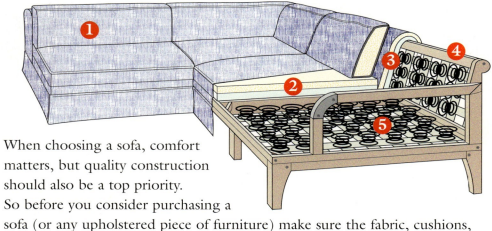

When choosing a sofa, comfort matters, but quality construction should also be a top priority. So before you consider purchasing a sofa (or any upholstered piece of furniture) make sure the fabric, cushions, padding, frame and deck meet the specifications below:

❶ The fabric If your sofa takes a lot of punishment, opt for a tightly woven fabric like rayon chenille or other synthetic blends. Also make sure, the fabric was treated at the mill with a stain-repellent finish, rather than having it sprayed on the finished sofa at the furniture store.

❷ The cushions The best back and seat cushions are made from high-density foam rubber, which provides support and also lasts the longest. Cushions should weigh about 1.8 pounds per square inch or more; if you don't see this information on the sofa's tag, ask a salesperson.

❸ The padding At least two-inches of padding should cover the frame for maximum comfort and to protect fabric from fraying.

❹ The frame A well-constructed sofa should have a frame that's made of kiln-dried hardwood, such as oak, maple or ash. The frame should be joined with dowels and corner blocks that are both glued and screwed for strength.

❺ The deck Ask a salesperson whether your choice of sofa has hand-tied coils and cone springs for adequate support and extra resilience.

UNIT 4

🎧 12 A house-warming party

After Patricia has finally moved into her new home she decides to have a party.

TIM Do you know all these people here, Patricia? I don't know anyone here, except you.

PATRICIA I know some of them. The tall one with straight dark brown hair is Harald. He lives here.

TIM He's the student from Austria, isn't he?

PATRICIA Yes, he is. And the red-haired girl over there is Sheila, the one with the pony tail.

TIM Oh yes, you told me about her. She works at St. Andrew's hospital, doesn't she?

PATRICIA Yes, that's right. And the short slim one with curly hair is Sally King. But you've met her already, don't you remember? About two weeks ago, on the underground?

TIM Oh yes, but she looks different now, doesn't she?

PATRICIA Yes, she's had her hair dyed.

TIM And who is she talking to? The black guy with the moustache?

PATRICIA That's David, he lives here too.

TIM Oh, yes, the computer expert. You told me about him. What happened to him? He's got his arm in plaster.

PATRICIA He had an accident on his bicycle a few days ago and broke his arm, poor guy.

Do these tasks.

1 Read or listen to the dialogue and look at the picture. Can you identify the people Patricia describes?
2 Describe the other people on the picture.
3 Describe people in your class.

UNIT 5 | Kitchen equipment

1 A telephone message

Alan Macintosh works at Barnes Home and Furnishing. While he is out of the shop one day, the phone rings in his department. Listen to the telephone call and write down a message for him.

☎ MESSAGE ☎

From _____ To _____
Date _____ Time _____
Message

ALPHABET AND INTERNATIONAL SPELLING CODE

A	ay	Alpha		N	enn	November
B	bee	Bravo		O	oh	Oscar
C	see	Charlie		P	pee	Papa
D	dee	Delta		Q	queue	Quebec
E	ee	Echo		R	are	Romeo
F	eff	Foxtrot		S	ess	Sierra
G	gee	Golf		T	tee	Tango
H	aytch	Hotel		U	you	Uniform
I	eye	India		V	vee	Victor
J	jay	Juliette		W	double-you	Whisky
K	kay	Kilo		X	ex	X-ray
L	ell	Lima		Y	why	Yankee
M	emm	Mike		Z	zed (AE: zee)	Zulu

2 Spelling

In pairs, practise spelling. Student A look at this page and dictate the names and addresses to your partner. Student B look at File 5 on page 98.

Barbra E. Davidge
447 Wisteria Circle
Redhill
RH1 4NA

Jill G. Quaill
89 Kingsford Avenue
Peterborough PE13 4DG

Vijay Rajagopal
1235 Maude Court
Simsbury, CT 06070

37

3 Ordering by phone

One day a customer calls Barnes Home and Furnishing to place an order for some tableware she's seen in a catalogue. Draw an order form like the one below in your exercise book. Then complete it with information from the telephone conversation.

Barnes Home and Furnishing
44 HIGH GATE LONDON NW67PB

Order Form

Name and address

Mr/Ms/Mrs/Ms _____

Address _____

_____

_____

_____

Postcode _____

Telephone number _____

Description	Reference number	Quantity	Item price	Total price

Subtotal _____
Delivery charge _____
Total _____

Payment: Credit card (number/expiry date) Cheque/COD

Dinner plate
Diameter 28cm
43517K 1   £5

Dessert Plate
Diameter 22cm
43643G   £4

Bowl
Diameter 22cm
43437L   £4,30

Mug
Height 9.5cm
43381X   £3,50

Salt Mill
43450H   £6

Pepper Mill
43187A   £6

Covered Vegetable Dish
Diameter 23cm, 1.8 Litres
43832B 3   £7,50

Gravy Boat and Stand
43658E   £6,50

Salad Bowl
Diameter 25cm
43802I   £8,50

Tablecloth
100 % cotton.
183 x 127cm.
43438Y   £10

Napkins
Pack of four. 100 % cotton. 43 x 43cm
43336J   £6

Oval Platter
Length 41cm
43876W   £9

Teapot
Capacity four cups.
43987R   £10

Milk Jug
43123V   £8

Tea Cup and Saucer
43876Q   £5

4 Working with words

Complete the sentences with the words below.

> broken ◆ case ◆ cash ◆ charge ◆ come ◆ connect ◆ happen
> items ◆ right ◆ spell ◆ stock ◆ take

1 Hold on a minute, I'll … you to our china and crockery department.
2 I'd like to order some … from your Summertime collection if that's possible.
3 Do you … to know the reference number?
4 I've got the catalogue … here.
5 Two of my cups are … . Can I buy cups without saucers?
6 No, I'm sorry, they … as a set, you see.
7 Could you … your name and address, please?
8 Could you give me your phone number just in … we need to contact you?
9 The delivery … will be £3 because the total amount is under £100.
10 You can give me your credit card number or you can pay … on delivery.
11 How long will it …?
12 If everything is in … you'll have the goods within three or four days.

5 Practice

Look again at the list of items in exercise 3. In pairs, practise ordering by phone.

6 Household gadgets

Match the pictures with the descriptions.

1 coffee-maker
2 pressure cooker
3 food slicer
4 kettle
5 multi-purpose knife
6 pan set
7 food processor
8 toaster
9 tool set

The ...1 with 10-cup filter coffee capacity and thermos. Water level gauge. Permanent stainless steel filter. Safety pressure valve. Cord storage in base. 2 glass jugs and lids. £57.90.

Safety ...2 with large removable blade. Sliding food carriage with finger protection and food grip. Variable slicing control. Safety press and hold switch. Folding carriage – protects the blade and the slicer is stored safely and compactly. Cord storage. £29.50.

...3. Variable width facility for thick and thin bread. Electronic variable browning control. High-lift facility for small items. Extra deep toasting chamber. Removable crumb tray. Cord storage. £21.50

500 watt ...4. Detachable 2.7 pint blender attachment. 2 speeds pulse action. Dishwasher safe bowl. Chopping blade and 4 discs for shredding, slicing and chipping etc., citrus press. 1.5 litre (2.6 pints) capacity. £89.99

...5. Sharp and tough, for slicing bread, meat, etc. Dishwasher-safe blades. Safety on/off switch £17.99

Rapid boil jug ...6 features a concealed element for easier cleaning and reduced limescale build-up. Water level indicator, cord storage and non-slip feet. 2.6 pints (1.5 litres) capacity. Available in blue, green and white. £37.99.

...7 set and rack. Comprises: spoon, soup ladle, turner, 2 sieves, whisk and grater on a rack. £4.25

Stainless steel ...8. Triple safety overpressure system. Lid safety locking device prevents opening of lid until all pressure is safely released. 6 litres (10.5 pints) capacity. Suitable for gas and electric hobs. 10 year guarantee. Free cookbook. £59.99.

Five-piece-...9. Comprises 16cm, 20cm, 22cm and 30cm diam. saucepans with lids, milk pan. Dishwasher safe. Special base for superior heat distribution. Stainless steel. £69.99

40 UNIT 5

7 Customer questions

Read the descriptions again and answer the following questions.

1. What is the pressure cooker made of?
2. Do I use ordinary paper filters with the coffee-maker?
3. How can the food slicer be stored when it's not in use?
4. How much does the kettle hold?
5. Can any parts of the toaster be removed for cleaning?
6. Can I put any parts of the food processor in the dishwasher?
7. What kinds of things can I cut with the multi-purpose knife?
8. What kind of tools are there in the tool set?
9. What free gift do I get when I buy the pressure cooker?
10. What colour is the kettle available in?

8 Questions and answers

In pairs, make up 10 more questions and answers about the kitchen gadgets and equipment above.

GRAMMAR CHECK

MODAL VERBS AND THEIR SUBSTITUTES

1. The food processor **can** shred, slice and chip.
2. You **may** put the bowl in the dishwasher.
3. You **must not** scratch the inside of the saucepan with a knife.
4. You **will be able to** cook a dinner in a much shorter time.
5. He **had to** unplug the machine before he cleaned it.
6. We're sorry to **have to** inform you that the toaster is not available …

- *Hilfsverben* (modals) *haben in allen Personen dieselbe Form. Sie werden mit dem Infinitiv ohne* to *verwendet (1–3).*
- *Hilfsverben haben eine Gegenwartsform, manche auch eine eigene Vergangenheitsform. Ersatzverben* (substitutes) *werden benutzt, um andere Zeiten zu bilden (4, 5) bzw. wenn der Infinitiv benötigt wird (6). Beachten Sie folgende Übersicht:*

Hilfsverb	Ersatzverb	Entsprechung
can	be able to	können
could		konnten/könnten
may		könnten
may	be allowed to	dürfen
might		dürften
must not	not be allowed to	nicht dürfen
should / ought to		sollten
must	have to	müssen
need not	not have to	nicht müssen
		nicht brauchen

9 Practice

Put the modal verbs into the right tense. Use a substitute if necessary.

1 I phoned several shops to get a new jug for the coffee-maker, but I … (can/not) get the right one. *couldn't be able to*
2 Our toaster is broken, we … (must) get a new one soon. *will have to*
3 With this new knife you … (can) cut almost anything: food, metal, plastic… . *are able to*
4 Do you think I … (can) use her food slicer for the party next week? *will be able to*
5 The kettle did not work properly so we … (have to) take it back to the shop. *had*
6 I didn't know that glasses … (should/not) go in the dishwasher. *shouldn't*
7 I once had a food processor like that. You … (can) put the bowl in the dishwasher, so you … (not have to) wash it by hand. *could / didn't have to*

10 Practice

Complete the following sentences using 'need not' or 'must not'.

1 Tomorrow is her birthday. We … forget to buy her a present. *mustn't*
2 You … chop the onions with a knife. You can also use the food processor. *needn't*
3 He says we … help him, he can manage on his own. *needn't*
4 You … clean any electrical appliances when they are plugged in. It's dangerous. *mustn't*
5 Make sure you store the spices in a dry place. They … get wet. *mustn't*
6 We … pay for the delivery. It's included in the price. *needn't*
7 You … heat the pot when it's empty, you'll damage the non-stick layer. *mustn't*
8 You … pay now, you can do that when you pick up the goods. *needn't*

11 Working with words

Unscramble the words to find the matching nouns for the words below.

heghit ◆ erseprsu ◆ raterg ◆ dhitw ◆ ceilrs ◆ aegorst
bidiorstintu ◆ ydelrvei ◆ aefsty ◆ beldenr

1 blend *blender*
2 deliver *delivery*
3 distribute *distribution*
4 high *height*
5 grate *grater*
6 press *pressure*
7 safe *safety*
8 slice *slicer*
9 store *storage*
10 wide *width*

UNIT 5

12 A recipe

Choose the right words to complete the recipe (but check the CD before you start cooking!). Then list the equipment you would need to make the dish.

> cover ◆ cut ◆ cut ◆ garnish ◆ mix ◆ place ◆ place ◆ pour
> prepare ◆ put ◆ refrigerate ◆ remove ◆ stir ◆ whip

Sherry trifle

What you need

1 sponge cake
  16 cm diameter,
  3 cm deep
2/3 cup sherry
1/2 cup boiling water
1 packet red jelly
2/3 cup cold water
1/2 cup sugar
1/2 cup custard powder (vanilla flavour)
2 1/2 cups milk
1 egg
2 cans of peach slices, drained
1 cup cream
1/2 cup icing sugar
250 g strawberries

What you do

1 ...^{1} sponge cake into 2 cm cubes and ...^{2} in serving dish. Drizzle sherry over the cake.

2 ...^{3} boiling water over jelly crystals and ...^{4} until dissolved. Add cold water. Pour into a large tin and refrigerate until set.

3 ...^{5} the custard according to the instructions on the packet. ...^{6} from heat, add the egg and ...^{7} well. ...^{8} surface with plastic wrap, cool to room temperature.

4 ...^{9} jelly into cubes. ...^{10} in a layer on top of the sponge. Add fruit for the next layer, then pour custard over top. ...^{11} for at least 20 minutes.

5 ...^{12} cream with icing sugar and ...^{13} decoratively onto trifle and ...^{14} with strawberries.

13 Puzzle

Copy this table onto a separate piece of paper. Then fill it in with the 11 other kitchen gadgets and equipment hidden in the puzzle.

N	A	P	G	N	I	Y	R	F	K	B
S	E	L	T	T	E	K	B	N	W	L
T	O	A	S	T	E	R	I	L	M	E
S	F	O	R	K	C	F	X	A	M	N
F	C	U	T	L	E	R	Y	D	A	D
W	F	G	S	P	O	O	N	L	S	E
H	K	J	L	L	R	H	G	E	H	R
C	O	F	F	E	E	M	A	K	E	R
F	O	O	D	S	L	I	C	E	R	S
S	C	I	S	S	O	R	S	M	Y	E

electric	non-electric
coffee-maker	scissors

UNIT 6 | Electrical appliances and equipment

1 Whose job is it?

Look at this list of household chores. Do you think they should be done most often by a woman or by a man, or should they be shared equally if a couple live together?

Then read the analysis. Discuss the results in class.

	man	woman	shared
cleaning windows	b	a	c
cooking	b	a	c
drilling holes in the wall	a	b	c
dusting	b	a	c
changing electric bulbs	a	b	c
ironing	b	a	c
repairing dripping taps	a	b	c
sewing on buttons	b	a	c
shopping	b	a	c
vacuum-cleaning	b	a	c
washing	b	a	c
washing-up	b	a	c

Mainly a

You stick very much to the traditional roles. Nowadays most women have a full-time job and it is not right to expect them to do the full-time job of a housewife as well. On the other hand, a man who is unable to do necessary household chores is helpless when he wants to or has to live alone. There are certain things everyone should know about and that is true for men and women. Using an electric drill is just as simple as turning on a washing-machine and vice versa.

Mainly b

You would like to change the traditional roles of men and women in the home, but you should be aware that just reversing the expectations of men and women — for example, expecting men to do all the ironing and dusting or women to change all the electric bulbs — will not solve any of the problems. Perhaps you should look for a more flexible solution — for example, if a man is good at cooking, then he should cook most of the meals, but if he prefers doing the washing-up, then maybe he should do that instead.

Mainly c

You know that housework is something that has to be done, whether you like it or not. You may find one job better than the other, or at least not quite as bad, and you may be able to find a compromise. Sharing unloved chores can be a good basis for a happy relationship.

44

2 Progress dishwasher

IMAGINE how much time you'd save every day if you didn't have to wash up, especially if you have a large family. With a dishwasher you'd never have to do this daily chore again and you'd have more time to spend on the things you want to do. Save up to 500 hours per year at the kitchen sink – that's almost 3 solid weeks!

- The Progress DF 2000 dishwasher combines top-class performance with minimum energy (1.6 kWh/cycle), water and detergent consumption.
- It has six different programmes to choose from, including economy, delicate, half-load and HPS (High Performance System uses a double power jet to remove dried-on food).
- The DF 2000 is also extremely quiet in operation, at just 48 decibels.
- Measuring 60 cm wide, the Progress DF 2000 will take 12 place settings. The well-planned interior includes two folding shelves for cups and small glasses.
- The dishwasher is simple to operate and has the additional features of a child-safety catch and an anti-flood system.
- The stainless steel interior is guaranteed rust-free.
- Extended guarantee (3 years).

Read the text about the dishwasher and respond to the customers' questions.

1. We're not usually at home during the day. Can we turn it on in the evening or do you think it will be very loud?

2. Wouldn't it be dangerous if our little boy tried to open it?

3. Do you think we really need a dishwasher? There are only two of us.

4. Doesn't it use a lot of energy?

5. There are six people in our family and usually we're all at home for breakfast and dinner. How often would we have to run it?

6. What about a guarantee?

GRAMMAR CHECK

IF SENTENCES TYPE 2

1 If we **bought** a dishwasher, we **would save** a lot of time.
2 If we **ordered** it today, they **could deliver** it next week.
3 If I **were** you, I **would take** this one.
4 We **would buy** a dishwasher if our kitchen **were/was** not so small.

- *If-Sätze (Type 2) drücken mögliche, aber nicht sichere Ereignisse aus (1–4).*
- *Beachten Sie die Zeitenfolge: Der if-Nebensatz steht im* simple past *und im Hauptsatz wird* would + Infinitiv *verwendet (1). Would kann durch* could, might *oder* should *ersetzt werden (2). Das Wort* was *im if-Nebensatz wird manchmal durch* were *ersetzt (3, 4).*
- *Steht der if-Nebensatz an erster Stelle, wird er vom Hauptsatz durch ein Komma getrennt (1–3).*

3 Practice

Form if sentences as shown in the example.

EXAMPLE If you … (clean) the windows, I … (vacuum) the carpet.
If you cleaned the windows, I could vacuum the carpet.

1 If he … (do) the dusting, she … (do) the ironing.
2 If we … (have) a dishwasher, we … (not/have) to wash up by hand anymore.
3 If we … (want) it delivered next week, we … (have) to order it now.
4 She … (not/hang) up the clothes on the line if she … (have) a tumble-dryer.
5 If they … (know) more about repairing things, they … (do) a lot of things themselves.
6 You … (save) electricity and washing powder if you only … (turn) on the washing machine when it was full.

4 What would you do if …?

What would or could you do if …? Make sentences with the words below.

1 work in a restaurant
2 have more time for myself
3 be a teacher
4 have a family of my own
5 earn 10 times more than I do now
6 be the boss of a company
7 live in London
8 have a flat of my own

5 On test – Appliances you can rely on

Read the newspaper article and answer the question on page 48.

46 UNIT 6

An at a glance guide to the most and least reliable brands of 9 major appliances. To help you choose wisely we highlight the most common problems which these machines have and point out the brands which are most likely to suffer from them. Our guide to the most reliable appliances is based on the experiences of thousands of readers who told us their machines had broken down in the previous 12 months. From this we have built up a picture of which brands are more or less likely to need repairs. For each appliance we rank brands as 'most reliable', 'average' or 'least reliable'.

	Test result	Most reliable	Average	Least reliable
1	One in 12 tumble-dryers developed a fault in the 12 months covered by our survey.	Berillo Horizon	Dash Exon Knight	Floyd
2	One in 9 colour televisions in our survey developed a fault.	Console Genius	Berillo Irena	Arizon
3	One in eight VCRs had a fault.	Jasper	Arizon Genius	Irena
4	Washing machines are one of the least reliable appliances around – one in five needed a repair in the previous year. Water leaks account for more than a quarter of all faults.		Horizon Knight	Floyd Dash
5	These dual-function wash-dryers are even less reliable than washing machines. The most common problem was water leaking from the machine. The second most common problem was the machine making unusual noises.		Dash Horizon	Exon Floyd
6	One in six dishwashers had a repair in the previous year. The machine stopping before the end of a program and water leaking from the machine each accounted for one in six of all faults with dishwashers.	Dash	Berillo Floyd Horizon	Exon Knight
7	Cylinder cleaners develop fewer faults than uprights. One in five uprights and one in seven cylinders developed a fault in the previous year.	Berillo Knight	Horizon	Floyd
8	Microwave ovens were the most reliable type of appliance in our survey. Just one in 20 had a fault.	Berillo Floyd Knight	Dash Horizon Exon	
9	These appliances are also very reliable. One in 24 chest freezers, one in 16 upright freezers and one in ten fridge freezers developed a fault each year.	Berillo Exon	Dash Floyd Knight	

Answer the questions.

1. What is the test based on?
2. What is the most reliable make of dishwasher?
3. What is the least reliable make of tumble-dryer?
4. What is the difference between the two types of vacuum cleaner?
5. What are the most common problems with dishwashers?
6. Which is the most reliable type of domestic appliance?
7. Which are the least reliable types of domestic appliances?
8. Comparing the different types of fridges and freezers, which is the most reliable?

COMPARISON OF ADJECTIVES

as few as	fewer than	fewest
as reliable as	more / less reliable than	best
as good as	better than	most / least reliable
not so bad as	worse than	worst

6 Practice

Compare the electrical appliances by putting in the correct forms of the words in brackets. Look at the examples before starting.

EXAMPLES Horizon tumble-dryers are (good/...) Berillo but Floyd is the (bad) of all makes.
Horizon tumble-dryers are as good as Berillo but Floyd is the worst of all makes.

Microwave ovens are nearly (reliable/...) fridges and freezers.
Microwave ovens are nearly as reliable as fridges and freezers.

1. (Few) Horizon washing machines needed a repair (...) Floyd and Dash washing machines.
2. Of the problems with wash-dryers, water leaking was even (common/...) unusual noises.
3. Upright vacuum cleaners usually need repairs (often/...) cylinder cleaners.
4. The (reliable) of all appliances are microwave ovens.
5. Exon and Floyd are the (bad) wash-dryers, they are (bad/...) Dash and Horizon.
6. Of the colour TVs, Berillo are (good/...) Irena, (good/...) Arizon but not (good/...) Consule and Genius.

7 Practice

Write five more sentences like the ones in exercise 6.

8 What do you do if …?

Match the sentences on the left with the responses on the right.

1 The radio is too loud. Switch it off.
2 I want to watch a programme on TV. Turn it down.
3 There is smoke coming out of the TV. Switch it on.
4 The dishwasher has finished the programme. Plug it in.
5 The cooker is too hot. Switch it on.
6 I want to use my computer. Turn it down.
7 I want to use the iron. I want to iron a linen shirt. Unplug it.
8 Now I want to iron a silk scarf. Switch it off.
9 I don't need the iron any more. Turn it down
10 I don't want to watch TV any more. Unplug it.

9 Operating instructions

Student A look below and use the information to answer Student B's questions. Student B look at File 3 on page 97.

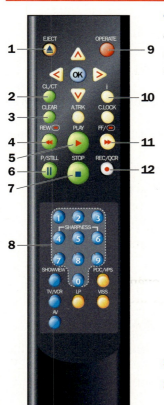

The Remote Control Handset

This video recorder is designed so that almost all of its functions can be controlled from the remote control handset. This must have a 'line of sight' to the sensor on the front of the video recorder.

1 **EJECT** To eject a tape.

2 **CLOCK/TAPE COUNTER** To switch the display on the front panel of the video recorder between the current time and the tape counter (in hours and minutes). This function will only operate when a tape is loaded.

3 **CLEAR** To reset the tape counter to zero.

4 **REW** To rewind the tape. To see reverse playback picture at high speed.

5 **PLAY** To play the tape.

6 **P/STILL** Switches to still picture, during recording to pause.

7 **STOP** To stop the tape.

8 **NUMBER BUTTONS** To select programme channels.

9 **OPERATE** To switch the video recorder on and off.

10 **CHILD LOCK** To turn the child lock function on/off.

11 **FF** To wind the tape forward. To see forward playback picture at high speed.

12 **REC/QSR** Used to record and set the QSR (Quick Set Recording) time.

UNIT 7 | Beauty for sale

1 At the chemist's

ASSISTANT	You said two bottles of shampoo, didn't you?
BRENDA	Yes, please.
ASSISTANT	Here you are, madam. Anything else?
BRENDA	Yes, I need a day cream for sensitive skin. Do you sell Sanson cosmetics?
ASSISTANT	No, I'm sorry, we don't sell that brand. But may I show you something similar? Albaline, for instance, is a range of products that we've been selling a lot of lately. Here's a tester if you'd like to have a try.
BRENDA	Yes, thank you. Oh, it smells very nice, doesn't it?
ASSISTANT	Yes, it's made with aloe and peach extracts. They only use natural ingredients and they don't test on animals.
BRENDA	They don't test on animals? Do you mean the others do?
ASSISTANT	Well, many cosmetics and also detergents and things like that are tested on animals.
BRENDA	Really? Medicines are often tested on animals, aren't they? But cosmetics? I didn't know that.
ASSISTANT	You know, not many people do. But there is an increasing number of firms now that don't test on animals. It really isn't necessary, is it? There are some quite sensible alternatives. Here's a brochure from the Anti-Vivisection Campaign if you'd like to have a look.
BRENDA	Yes, thank you. That's very interesting.

> **CAREFUL!**
> sensitive = empfindlich, sensibel
> sensible = vernünftig

Read the text and find the English translations of the following words.

1 empfindlich
2 Marke
3 ähnlich
4 zum Beispiel
5 Inhaltsstoffe
6 Kosmetik(a)
7 Reinigungsmittel
8 steigend
9 vernünftig
10 Aktion gegen Tierversuche

2 Who's right?

BRENDA Cecil, look at what I got in the shop today. It's a pamphlet against animal testing. It's really interesting, isn't it?

CECIL I just don't understand these people. What do they want? Companies can't try out their stuff on humans, can they?

BRENDA But all that testing is very cruel. And it's not always necessary, is it? I do feel sorry for the poor creatures.

CECIL Come on, Brenda, you wouldn't like to be the guinea-pig for a new medicine, would you? And what about medical students? They have to practise operations, don't they? You wouldn't want them to practise on humans, would you?

BRENDA It's not only medicines and operations, Cecil. Cosmetics and detergents are tested as well. And every time a new product comes onto the market some poor animals have to suffer.

CECIL But there is no other way, is there? Cosmetics and detergents can cause awful allergies. You know that as well as I do, don't you?

BRENDA Well, yes. But firstly, rabbits don't necessarily have the same allergies as people. And secondly, there are alternatives. What some companies do, it says here, is mainly use old, reliable ingredients that have been proven safe. And quite often they can do in vitro tests that do not involve the use of animals.

Read or listen to the dialogue above and write down Brenda's and Cecil's arguments in a table like the one below. Which do you agree with?

Brenda	Cecil
Animal tests are so cruel ...	*They can't try out the products on humans ...*

3 Arguments

Work with a partner, and use the phrases in the box to tell each other your opinions on animal testing.

> **GIVING YOUR OPINION**
>
> I'm sure that … / It's quite probable that …
> I think that … / I'd say that …
> As far as I know … / I'm not sure if …
> It's possible that … / I believe that …
> I suppose that … / In my opinion …
> On the one hand …, on the other hand …

GRAMMAR CHECK

QUESTION TAGS

1. You said two bottles, **didn't you**?
2. It smells very nice, **doesn't it**?
3. They can't try out their stuff on humans, **can they**?
4. You wouldn't like that, **would you**?

- *Man verwendet Satzanhängsel, wenn man eine Bestätigung einer Aussage erwartet.*
- *Ein verneintes Anhängsel wird an einen bejahten Aussagesatz angehängt (1, 2), ein bejahtes an einen verneinten Aussagesatz (3, 4).*

4 Practice

Use a suitable question tag to complete the following questions.

1. That brochure is very interesting, …?
2. But it's not all true, …?
3. They are tested on animals, …?
4. It was made of natural ingredients, …?
5. The tests were necessary, …?
6. You like that brand, …?
7. But you don't know Albaline, …?
8. She doesn't buy this skin cream, …?
9. They bought a bottle of shampoo, …?
10. But they didn't like it very much, …?
11. You've never heard of that before, …?
12. She will use something else next time, …?
13. Students must practise operations, …?
14. But we wouldn't like to be the guinea pigs, …?
15. You can understand her opinion, …?

5 Beauty for sale

Find the right word for each beauty product in the puzzle.

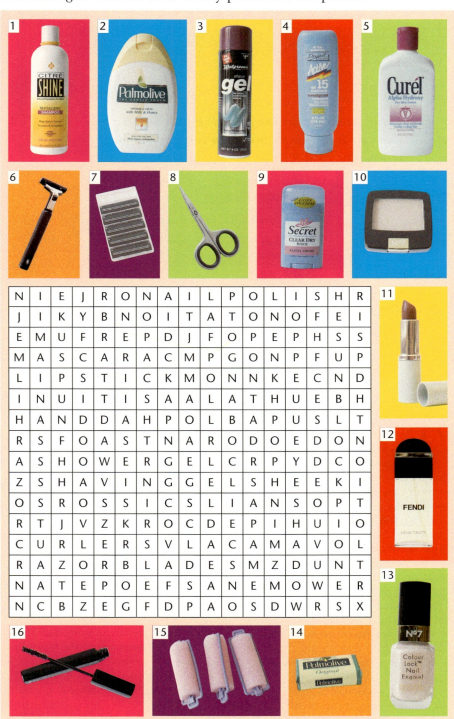

6 Skincare products

Read the following brochure. Then try to answer the customers' questions.

SKINCARE for TEENAGERS

Using products that are properly formulated for your skin type is very important. You can analyze your skin with a good light and a mirror.

SKIN TYPE	SKIN CHARACTERISTICS
very dry	Dry all over, tight, easily irritated.
normal to dry	Normal to oily in the T-zone, dry on the sides of the face.
normal	Slightly oily in the T-zone, normal on the sides of the face.
normal to oily	Oily in the T-zone, normal to oily on the sides of the face.
oily	Very oily in the T-zone, slightly oily on the sides of the face.
very oily / blemished	Very oily all over, with frequent problem breakouts.

There are some basics that all teens should follow to help keep skin 'normal'. You should use a cleanser, rather than soap, to wash your face. Soap can overdry the surface of your skin and cause it to feel oily in just a few hours.

Wash your face morning and night (at least) and follow with a toner (preferably one that doesn't contain alcohol). Wash your face at night to remove the dirt and pollution (and make-up) from your skin. During the night, your skin remains active, even while you rest, and you should wash again in the morning to start with clear skin.

Use a moisturizer every day (even if you have oily skin – just use one that is oil-free). This helps protect your skin from the dirt and pollution in the air.

If you have blemishes and use a blemish cream or lotion, use a cotton wool bud and only treat the blemish itself (not the surrounding area). This dries the blemish, not the skin around it. Don't pick at blemishes and do try to keep your hands off your face.

Regular use of a face mask that is appropriate for your skin type further helps to balance your skin and helps 'tighten' pores. To make this easier, apply the mask and let it dry for 5-10 minutes before your shower (the mask is easier to remove in the shower).

Regular use of a scrub (gently please, you don't want to irritate your skin) helps deep clean your skin and makes your complexion look brighter and clearer. If you have spots, be very careful using a scrub, because the grains can irritate the blemishes and make them worse. Gently apply the scrub to your damp skin and gently rinse off. The scrub also helps fight blackheads and tighten pores.

1 Why shouldn't I wash my face with soap?
2 Why should I wash my skin at night?
3 Why should I use a moisturizer?
4 How should I treat blemishes?
5 What does the regular use of a face mask do for my skin?
6 How should I apply the mask?
7 Why should I use a scrub?
8 Why should I be careful when using a scrub?

7 Cleopatra's secret

Something was spilled on this recipe for an Egyptian face mask. Listen to the CD to find the missing words.

Ingredients

1 beaten …1
½ teaspoon …2
1 tablespoon …3
½ teaspoon sea …4
1 tablespoon whole …5

Mix all …6 until they are thoroughly blended. Spread the mixture over your face and neck and leave it on for about 15 minutes. Rinse well with …7 and pat dry.

8 Working with words

Find the most suitable word to complete each sentence.

> advantage ◆ brand ◆ brochure ◆ detergent ◆ fortunately
> ingredients ◆ instance ◆ sensible ◆ sensitive ◆ similar ◆ suffer

1 A large number of animals … for beauty.
2 Be careful what you say to him, he can be very … .
3 I can give you a … about skin care. You can read it at home.
4 It is very simple to make that cake; just mix all the … in a bowl.
5 It was very … of you to lock the door properly.

6 Sarah and her sister look very … . You can hardly tell who is who.
7 Sarah had a car accident yesterday; …, she was only slightly injured.
8 She speaks two foreign languages, that's a great … in her career.
9 They are all natural products, this one here, for …, is made with blackberry.
10 This a very famous …, that's why it is so expensive.
11 You can clean it with a mild … .

9 Opposites

Unscramble the words in the box to find the opposites of the words in the list.

1 easy
2 clean
3 active
4 gentle
5 interesting
6 similar
7 resistant
8 dry
9 artificial
10 expensive
11 awful
12 increase

10 Odd word out

Which word does not belong with the others? Give a reason why.

1 face ◆ curlers ◆ hand ◆ body
2 wash ◆ rinse ◆ complexion ◆ shower
3 moisturizer ◆ dirt ◆ pollution ◆ dust
4 remove ◆ bottle ◆ remain ◆ rinse
5 shampoo ◆ comb ◆ razor ◆ curlers
6 scissors ◆ blusher ◆ eye shadow ◆ lipstick
7 sensitive ◆ dry ◆ oily ◆ sunblock
8 soap ◆ pollution ◆ scrub ◆ mask
9 mirror ◆ blemish ◆ blackhead ◆ pore
10 cream ◆ lotion ◆ cotton wool bud ◆ oily

UNIT 8 | A green world

1 How much do you care?

Test yourself and discuss the results in class. Give reasons for your answers.

EXAMPLES Sometimes I buy mercury-free batteries but usually I use batteries that can be recharged.
I often buy soft drinks in aluminium cans but I always return them for recycling.
I never use public transport because it's so slow.

How often do you

often   *never*

1. buy environmentally friendly aerosols?
2. buy free-range chicken or eggs?
3. buy toiletries or cosmetics not tested on animals?
4. return bottles, tins, newspapers etc for recycling?
5. buy environmentally friendly washing powders/detergents?
6. choose to eat less meat?
7. choose products made of recycled materials?
8. refuse unnecessary packaging or wrapping?
9. buy organically grown fruit and vegetables?
10. buy mercury-free batteries?
11. use public transport?
12. buy CFC (chlorofluorocarbons) blown/polystyrene foam like fast food packaging?

sometimes   *sometimes*

often   *never*

2 Organic food

Katie Richmond is a shop assistant in a supermarket. Here she is talking to her manager, Ms Brown.

KATIE May I ask you something, Ms Brown?

MS BROWN Certainly, Katie, what would you like to know?

KATIE We have quite a lot of food that's labelled 'organically grown'. What exactly does that mean? Customers sometimes ask me about these products and I don't really know what to say.

MS BROWN 'Organically grown' means that the food is grown and processed without the use of synthetic fertilizers or pesticides.

KATIE How can that be proved? Isn't it possible that farmers lie about that? After all, organic food is more expensive.

MS BROWN Well, the farmers are members of organizations which certify that the products are OK.

KATIE How can they certify that?

MS BROWN The tests are quite strict. First the soil is tested to check that there are no remains of pesticides that had been used before. It takes a couple of years before a field is more or less free of pesticides, you see. Then the fields are inspected regularly to check that the farmers have not been using any forbidden substances.

KATIE What about animal products? You know, free-range chickens and all that?

MS BROWN Most hens are locked up in small cages and live in terrible conditions. But free-range chickens must have a certain amount of space outside to run around freely, I think it's about one square metre for each chicken or something like that. The same is true for cows. They must be allowed to go outside at least sometimes and must not be locked up all the time.

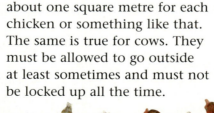

KATIE   And can we really be sure that there is no cheating?
MS BROWN   Well, we can never be a hundred per cent certain that everyone is honest. But we can guarantee that the products are tested and the majority of the products certainly are what they claim to be.

Read the dialogue again and answer the questions.
1 What is the difference between organically grown food and food grown by conventional methods?
2 How can it be proved that goods are organically grown?
3 What is tested?
4 How do free-range chickens live?
5 Is there a guarantee that there is no cheating?

3 Working with words

Find words in the dialogue which fit the following definitions.
1 grown in a natural way
2 artificial substances that make plants grow faster
3 something that is left over
4 chemical substance used to kill weeds or insects
5 hens kept in natural conditions
6 not allowed
7 always telling the truth
8 opposite of minority

4 Buying eggs

Customer

Sagen Sie, Sie möchten Eier kaufen.

Fragen Sie, was der Unterschied zu normalen Eiern ist.

Fragen Sie, ob die Freilandeier teurer sind.

Fragen Sie, wer garantiert, dass es wirklich Freilandeier sind.

Kaufen Sie 6 Eier.

Shop assistant

Fragen Sie, ob er/sie Freilandeier möchte.

Sagen Sie, dass die Hühner im Freien herumlaufen können und nicht eingesperrt sind.

Sagen Sie, dass sie ein bisschen teurer sind.

Sagen Sie, dass Ihr Geschäft die Eier direkt von den Bauern bezieht und diese kontrolliert werden.

5 GE foods

The paragraphs of this text are mixed up. Put them in the correct order.

Messing about with nature

B
Genetic engineering means altering the genes. But what is it all about? Genes are clumps of information about how to make parts of living bodies – a bit like the recipes for a cake. And every cell of every body of every living thing has this genetic code inside it. Genes sometimes can change. They do not always make perfect copies when a cell divides. This 'mistake' is

D
going on for millions of years, people want results fast. And big companies want to make lots of money out of GE. And there are always some people who don't care much. But GE is a risky business and nobody knows what will happen if most people eat GE food most of the time. Nor does anyone know what effect growing all these plants with altered genes will have on

A
could give an organism special new abilities like resisting a disease. Scientists that do GE tell us by making new types of organism they can make a plant grow bigger or faster. Others could be programmed to resist a disease. Some could even produce vaccines which could protect people against nasty illnesses. So, what is wrong with GE? While evolution has been

C
other plants or animals over time. The companies say they want to feed all the world's starving people. That is hard to believe. Few companies want to give money away –which is what they would have to do to feed the starving. Hungry people have no money to buy food or land to grow it on. That is why they are hungry, not because there is not enough food.

E
called a mutation. Some mutations are useful and give the creature an advantage in life. This slow business of trying out new body shapes and styles has been going on for as long as life – it is called evolution. Now what is the point of messing around with genes? People are impatient. They want to make new types of life which will do new things. Changing the genes

6 What does that mean?

Now read the text in the correct order and find the English translations of the following German words:

1 ändern
2 Rezept
3 teilen
4 Fehler
5 nützlich
6 Geschöpf
7 Vorteil

8 Form
9 herumpfuschen
10 ungeduldig
11 Fähigkeit
12 Wissenschaftler
13 Krankheit
14 Impfstoff

15 schützen
16 böse, schlimm
17 Ergebnis
18 riskant
19 verhungern
20 schwer

7 Comprehension

Read the text once more and answer the following questions.

1 What are genes?
2 What is a mutation?
3 Why do scientists want to alter genes?
4 What are the advantages of GE?
5 What are the risks of GE?

8 What do you think?

Read or listen to these statements about GE food. Say whether you agree or disagree with them.

Ian: We don't know what side effects there may be for animals and people who eat GE food.

Maria: If plants are made resistant to disease, we will need fewer pesticides. That's a good thing, isn't it?

Jason: But it's dangerous. As soon as plants with altered genes spread in nature, there is no way to stop them.

Andrew: GE can help to feed the people in poor countries.

Georgia: Don't be silly. The companies who do GE are not interested in feeding the poor. They're only interested in making profit.

Cathy: Scientists are just playing with nature and who knows what diseases they are creating.

Patrick: People are always afraid of new technology. In former times people were afraid of planes and even telephones, weren't they?

AGREEING AND DISAGREEING

I agree (with you/him/her).
Yes, you're right. That's the way it is.
I'm not 100 per cent sure but I think that's right.

I'm sorry, I don't agree. / I disagree.
No, I'm sorry. That's wrong. I think …
I think that's a silly reason/argument.

9 Synonyms

Find the matching pairs of words that have the same or a similar meaning.

artificial   *disease*   **fault**
certify   *horrible*
guarantee   *illness*   **mistake**
room   *space*   *synthetic*   *terrible*

10 Going veggie?

In groups of four have a discussion about the rights and wrongs of eating meat. First study your profiles in the pairwork file (Student A turn to File 2 on page 97; Student B turn to File 4 on page 98; Student C turn to File 6 on page 98; Student D turn to File 8 on page 100.) Then use the arguments there to give your opinion and agree or disagree with the others in your group. Make notes in a table like the one below about what each person says.

Person	Arguments
A	
B	
C	
D	

PREFIXES AND SUFFIXES

Prefixes (opposites)

un- (unhappy)
in- (incorrect)
dis- (disappear)
non- (non-stop)

il- only before l (illegal)
im- only before m or p (immoral, impossible)
ir- only before r (irregular)

Suffixes to form adjectives

-al (central)
-ent/ant (different, pleasant)
-less (careless)
-y (hungry)

-ive (expensive)
-ful (careful)
-ic (organic)
-able/-ible (washable, possible)

Suffixes to form nouns

-ment (environment)
-ty/ity (safety, majority)
-ing (building)

-ance/ence (entrance, silence)
-ness (happiness)
-tion/ation/ition/sion (reduction, organization, definition, discussion)

11 Working with words

Find the opposite of the following words using the prefixes in the box. Use three of the new words in sentences.

| dis- ◆ il- |
| im- ◆ in- |
| ir- ◆ non- |
| un- |

1 patient
2 fair
3 regular
4 secure
5 mature
6 smoker
7 advantage
8 responsible
9 certain
10 honest
11 expensive
12 necessary
13 logical
14 agree
15 perfect

12 Puzzle

Find nouns related to the following adjectives and verbs in the puzzle.

add ◆ clever ◆ cruel ◆ decide ◆ end ◆ employ ◆ expensive ◆ friendly ◆ honest ◆ independent ◆ invite ◆ organize ◆ possible ◆ real

Then find adjectives related to the following nouns.

care ◆ nature ◆ pessimism ◆ reason ◆ sense ◆ tradition ◆ type

E	C	N	E	D	E	P	E	D	N	I	H	A	I	A	J
H	O	N	E	S	T	Y	O	E	L	B	I	S	N	E	S
K	O	R	G	A	N	I	Z	A	T	I	O	N	V	K	Z
S	S	E	N	I	L	D	N	E	I	R	F	W	I	M	R
T	Y	P	I	C	A	L	L	C	R	U	E	L	T	Y	E
S	S	E	N	R	E	V	E	L	C	Q	F	N	A	Q	A
C	I	T	S	I	M	I	S	S	E	P	N	V	T	C	L
R	E	A	S	O	N	A	B	L	E	Y	O	G	I	A	I
S	M	D	E	C	I	S	I	O	N	K	I	N	O	R	T
Y	S	E	S	N	E	P	X	E	G	H	T	I	N	E	Y
T	N	E	M	Y	O	L	P	M	E	D	I	D	N	F	R
N	A	T	U	R	A	L	G	E	X	N	D	N	Y	U	O
T	R	A	D	I	T	I	O	N	A	L	D	E	G	L	V
P	O	S	S	I	B	I	L	I	T	Y	A	X	W	B	I

UNIT 9 | At a jewellery shop

1 Looking for a present

Read or listen to the dialogue and answer the questions.

JASON   I'm looking for a present for my girlfriend, but I'm not sure what would be the right thing for her.
JEWELLER   How old is the young lady?
JASON   She'll be 20 next week. It's for her birthday.
JEWELLER   I see. Do you know what kind of jewellery she might like? A bracelet, or a necklace? Or perhaps a chain with a pendant?
JASON   She likes rings, at least she wears them a lot. But I don't know her size and, of course, I'd like to surprise her. Necklaces are expensive, aren't they?
JEWELLER   Not really, it depends what they are made of – silver, gold, with or without gemstones… If you'd like to take a look, I can show you what we have.
JASON   Hm, I'm not sure.
JEWELLER   OK then, what about earrings? Most women like earrings.
JASON   Yes, perhaps earrings would be a good idea.
JEWELLER   Are her ears pierced?
JASON   I think so – yes, I'm sure they are.
JEWELLER   All these over here are 20 carat gold, and these here are gold-plated silver, those are sterling silver and the ones over there are fashion jewellery made of hypo-allergenic steel. What is your girlfriend like? Is she elegant, sporty? Tall? Short?
JASON   She's quite sporty. She's tall and slim with short, dark hair.
JEWELLER   Perhaps she'd prefer a simple design then. This pair here would look great with short hair.
JASON   Yes, they're very pretty. How much are they?

1 Why does Jason want to buy his girlfriend a present?
2 Why doesn't he want to buy a ring?
3 Why doesn't he want to buy a necklace?
4 What does his girlfriend look like?

2 Items in a jewellery shop

Match the words with the pictures.

> alarm clock ◆ bangles ◆ brooch/pin ◆ cuff links ◆ hoop earrings
> necklace ◆ pearl necklace ◆ pendant ◆ stud earrings
> tie clip ◆ watch ◆ wedding rings

3 Getting a watch repaired

Put the dialogue in order. Then read it out with a partner.

Shop assistant	Customer
Unfortunately our watchmaker is not here today, but he ought to be here tomorrow. Could you leave your watch here till tomorrow afternoon?	How long will that take?
Certainly sir, if you'd like to have a look? I'll show you what we've got.	No, but it got wet. You know, I usually take it off when I go swimming, but yesterday I forgot.
Let me see. … I'm sorry, but it's not the battery. There's something else wrong with your watch. Did you perhaps drop it or something?	Yes, my watch isn't working. I think it just needs a new battery, though.
Good morning. Can I help you?	This one here looks nice. How much is it?
But that shouldn't matter. It's a water-resistant watch so you could even use it for diving. It must be something else. But I can have it repaired for you if you like.	No, I can't wait that long. I'm leaving tomorrow morning, you see. I think I'd better buy a new one. Have you got a nice inexpensive watch?

UNIT 9

4 True or false?

Are the following statements true or false? Correct the false statements.

1. The watch needs a new battery.
2. The customer did not drop the watch.
3. The customer forgot to take off the watch when he went swimming.
4. The watch mustn't get wet.
5. The watch can be repaired the same day.
6. The customer wants to have the watch repaired.
7. The customer doesn't want to spend a lot of money for a new watch.

> **LASSEN**
>
> *etwas machen lassen* = have/get something done
> I can **have** the watch **repaired** for you if you like.
> I **got** my car **repaired**.
>
> *(ver)lassen, zurücklassen, übrig lassen, wegfahren, weggehen* = leave
> He usually **leaves** the office at 5 o'clock.
> He **left** his keys on his desk.
> The bus **leaves** at half past 7.
>
> *lassen im Sinne von etwas erlauben oder als Aufforderung* = let (someone do something)
> Sarah didn't **let** him drive her car.   **Let's** start now.
>
> *jdn etwas tun lassen bzw. dazu bringen, etwas zu tun* = make someone do something
> The trainer **made** us run for one hour.

5 Translation

Translate the following sentences into German. Then close the book and translate them back into English. Compare them with the original sentences.

1. Can I leave the clock here until tomorrow?
2. Did you have your car washed?
3. Don't let the dog out.
4. She had her hair dyed.
5. Please don't leave me!
6. He made me do all the work alone.
7. The bus leaves in 10 minutes.
8. Let's all go to the party.
9. The teacher will make us take a test tomorrow.
10. We've eaten everything, there's nothing left.
11. You must have your watch repaired.

6 Setting the time

Read or listen to the dialogue. Find the right words for the numbers 1–6 on the illustration.

CUSTOMER   How do I set the time?
SHOP ASSISTANT   It's very easy actually. Use the winder to set the time and date. Pull it to the first click, and you can set the date by turning it clockwise. You'll see the number change in the small window on the right of the clockface. If you pull the winder to the second click, you can set the time. You should do that when the second hand is at the 12 o'clock position – otherwise the hands may not show the exact time. Just turn the winder until the minute hand and the hour hand are in the correct position.

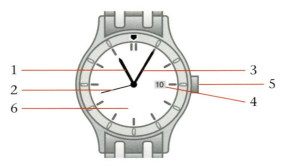

7 The power of stones

In pairs, look at the pictures of gemstones and try to label them with words from the list. Check your answers on pages 68 and 99.

lapis lazuli
hematite
topaz
jasper
amber
garnet
turquoise
emerald
rock crystal
opal
ruby
sapphire

Then student A look at the information on the next page, student B look at the information in File 7 on page 99. Read the texts and work together to answer the customers' questions.

THROUGHOUT HISTORY, gemstones have been said to have certain energies and healing qualities. Whether you believe in their secret powers or not, the simple beauty of precious and semi-precious stones makes them an elegant accessory for men and women. Here is a short guide to some of the most common stones.

- *Amber* releases tension, eases stress and can help you make the right decision. It is a good healing stone and is best worn as a bracelet or anklet. (photo 4)

- *Emerald* can help people who find it difficult to express themselves. This stone helps those who find it hard to give or receive love to break the barriers and to accept things more easily and joyfully. (photo 3)

- *Garnet* is good for people lacking confidence. It influences the world of imagination and dreams. It protects the bearer from negative thoughts and neutralizes fears and weaknesses. (photo 10)

- *Hematite* provides protection against negative emotions and increases resistance to stress. It is good for rational, logical people who do not rely on their senses and intuition. (photo 7)

- *Jasper* comes in different shades ranging from brown to red. This stone lends strength and determination to people in difficult situations. It symbolizes patience and tolerance. (photo 5)

- *Lapis Lazuli* is a very powerful stone and was the most common gemstone in ancient Egypt. It helps people to think more clearly and it is a very good stone for meditation. (photo 2)

1. I'm very stressed. Which stones should I wear?

2. I'd like to lose weight. Is there a stone which might help me?

3. My sister has a lot of problems at the moment. Are there any stones which could give her some extra strength or inner power?

4. It's my mother's birthday but she only wears red and brown stones. What should I buy her?

5. I'd like a stone which will help me feel more confident and less afraid. Do you have anything?

6. My girlfriend is very jealous. Is there a stone I could buy her to make her less jealous?

7. I love amber, but what is the best way to wear it?

8. I was given some turquoise earrings for my birthday. Does turquoise have any special qualities?

8 Puzzle

Copy this table onto a separate piece of paper. Then fill it in with words from the puzzle.

jewellery	gemstones

O	C	H	C	T	A	W	E	D	D	I	N	G	R	I	N	G	A	R	N
A	G	A	R	N	E	T	H	C	O	O	R	B	J	A	S	P	E	R	A
E	M	E	N	A	I	D	I	S	B	O	E	K	A	L	F	W	O	N	S
Z	A	P	O	T	R	I	T	R	P	E	N	D	A	N	T	U	Q	E	A
A	M	Z	A	I	N	E	A	A	Z	S	K	N	I	L	F	F	U	C	P
E	B	M	R	E	K	C	L	S	E	S	I	O	U	Q	R	U	T	K	P
R	E	E	Y	C	E	L	G	N	A	B	E	M	E	R	A	L	D	L	H
H	R	B	O	L	A	P	I	S	L	A	Z	U	L	I	A	R	B	A	I
T	U	L	E	I	S	G	N	I	R	R	A	E	D	U	T	S	M	C	R
R	Q	T	A	P	N	O	I	L	L	A	D	E	M	C	H	A	R	E	E

9 A burglary

Listen to the CD and find out who is who. What was each person doing when the burglary took place?

Natalie Thompson ◆ Charles McGyre ◆ Sharon Graham
Nancy Taylor ◆ Alistair O'Neil ◆ George Shepherd

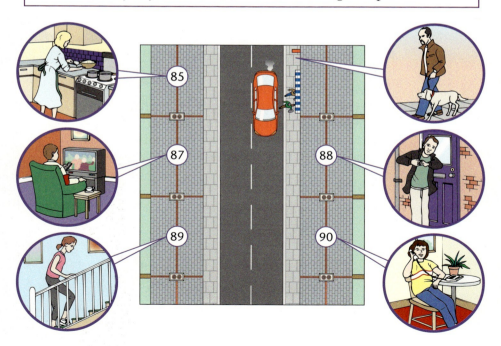

UNIT 9

GRAMMAR CHECK

PAST CONTINUOUS AND SIMPLE PAST

1 I **was preparing** supper when I **heard** a strange noise outside.
2 I **was taking** the dog for a walk and then suddenly a blue car **drove** past me.
3 Someone **screamed** and then the alarm **sounded**.

- *Diese Sätze beziehen sich auf einen nicht abgeschlossenen Vorgang in der Vergangenheit, der von einem anderen Geschehen ‚unterbrochen' wird. Das* past continuous *verwendet man für den nicht abgeschlossenen Vorgang und das* simple past *für das Geschehen, das ihn unterbricht (1, 2).*
- *Folgen zwei Handlungen aufeinander, so stehen beide im* simple past *(3).*

10 Interview with the witnesses

A policeman has just interviewed some witnesses. Look at his notes and say what the people were doing at the time of the crime.

EXAMPLE   Mrs Natalie Thompson/makes supper/hears strange noise outside.
Mrs Natalie Thompson was making supper when she heard a strange noise outside.

1 Mr Alistair O'Neil/enters his house/blue car stops nearby
2 Mr Charles McGyre/watches TV/alarm goes off
3 Mrs Sharon Graham draws the curtains of the bedroom window/doesn't see anything suspicious
4 Mr George Shepherd walks down Burlington Lane/two men run out of the jewellery shop
5 Mrs Nancy Jones/talks to her sister on the phone/somewhere someone starts to scream

UNIT 10 House and home

1 At the DIY store

Match the descriptions to the pictures.

HAMMER/ROTARY DRILL. 2,200–2,800 rpm. Complete with three masonry bits, depth gauge, rubber backing pad, 5 sanding discs and wall plugs.

JIGSAW. 500–2,700 rpm. Adjustable base plate. Transparent shield for clear sight of cutting line.

FORK AND SPADE. Carbon steel head with polypropylene hand grip for strength. 10-yr guarantee.

PETROL MOWER. Steel blade, large capacity grass box, 5 cutting heights.

LEAD. For small to medium dogs up to 44 kgs. One-handed operation. Control trigger acts as brake and lock. Approx. 5 metres.

PRESSURE WASHER. Powerful 1350W motor, maximum volume 420 litres per hour, supplied with high pressure hose, two-piece lance and detergent pot.

140-PIECE HOUSEHOLD TOOL KIT. Comprises basic tools for general carpentry and DIY jobs around the house.

KETTLE BARBECUE. Useful for covered cooking. Enamelled housing, chrome cooking grid, two mobility wheels and wire base shelf.

71

2 Abbreviations

Read the descriptions and find the short forms of the following words.

1 do it yourself
2 revolutions per minute
3 approximately
4 kilograms
5 Watt
6 year

3 Can you help me?

Listen to five foreign customers and help them find what they need.

4 Buying a power drill

Listen to the dialogue and answer the questions.

SHOP ASSISTANT Can I help you?
CUSTOMER Yes, please, I'd like to buy a drill, but I don't know which one. There are so many different types. Can you give me some advice?
SHOP ASSISTANT Certainly. Well, there are corded and cordless power drills. The corded ones have greater power, but the cordless ones are ideal when you are away from mains power, like in the garden or on a ladder. And they can also be used as a screwdriver. Where would you mainly use the drill?
CUSTOMER Mainly at home. And I live in a rather new house with concrete walls. So I think I'd need quite a strong one.
SHOP ASSISTANT Yes, you would certainly need a corded hammer action drill.
CUSTOMER What exactly is hammer action?
SHOP ASSISTANT That's where the drill vibrates rapidly. You need that for drilling masonry or concrete. All these drills here are hammer action drills.
CUSTOMER But the prices vary a lot.
SHOP ASSISTANT Well, the higher the wattage the more powerful they are. It depends how often you would use it and how much money you would like to spend.
CUSTOMER I don't think I'm going to use it very often, maybe a couple of times a year. So I'd rather buy one that is not so expensive. Do I need to buy bits or are they included?

SHOP ASSISTANT   There is a set of bits included. But be careful to use the right ones. You need masonry bits if you want to drill holes in walls. These here are used for wood and these are used for steel.

1 What is the advantage of the corded power drills?
2 What are the advantages of the cordless power drills?
3 What can cordless power drills also be used for?
4 What type of walls does the customer have at home?
5 What does 'hammer action' mean?
6 What is the difference between the cheaper and the more expensive drills?
7 Why doesn't the customer want to spend too much?
8 What types of bits are included?

5 Dialogues

Look back at exercise 3 and work with a partner to make a dialogue. One of you take the role of one of the customers, the other take the role of the shop assistant.

GRAMMAR CHECK

THE POSSESSIVE FORM

1 This is **my brother's** mower.
2 This is **Chris's** power drill.
3 This is a **girls'** school.
4 This is a **children's** tool-kit.
5 I bought it at **Brown's**. (I bought it at Brown's DIY store.)
6 She went to the **chemist's**. (She went to the chemist's shop.)

Achtung auf die Aussprache!
Chris's ['krɪsəs]

- *Bei Substantiven wird 's (Apostroph + s) angehängt (1, 2).*
- *Bei Substantiven im Plural wird ein Apostroph an die s-Endung des Plurals angehängt (3).*
- *Bei Substantiven im Plural, die nicht auf s enden (children, men) wird 's (Apostroph + s) angehängt (4).*
- *In Ortsbezeichnungen wird normalerweise das Substantiv nach dem s-Genitiv weggelassen (5, 6).*
- *Aber Vorsicht! Im Englischen zeigt der Apostroph auch an, dass ein oder mehrere Buchstaben ausgelassen worden sind, wie z. B. bei* don't (= do not) *oder* they're (= they are).

⚠ it's = it is, *aber* its *bedeutet ‚sein(e)' oder ‚ihr(e)'.*

UNIT 10

6 Practice

Look at these signs and correct any mistakes.

7 Practice

Rewrite the sentences using the full form of the words.

1. I'd like to buy a drill.
2. I don't think I'm going to use it very often.
3. It's quite expensive.
4. She can't decide what to buy.
5. He's just bought a new jigsaw.
6. The lead's nice. I think I'll buy it.
7. She doesn't like the pressure washer.
8. He didn't buy the expensive one.
9. He said he wouldn't need it.
10. They're at the DIY store at the moment.
11. They won't be open tomorrow.
12. I thought he'd bought a new barbecue.

8 What pet would suit you?

A society for the protection of animals has put the following quiz on their website. Work with a partner to take the quiz and find out what pet would suit you.

1 Do you work full-time?
a No
b Yes, I work shifts, sometimes at night
c Yes
d Yes, work is my life.

2 Do you have children?
a No
b At weekends
c Yes
d No, they take up too much time.

3 Have you had pets before?
a Yes
b Only as a child
c No
d Is a computer a pet?

4 Do you like exercise?
a Yes
b Sometimes
c No
d What is exercise?

5 What sort of home do you live in?
a House with a garden
b Flat or apartment
c House without a garden
d My office is my home.

6 You enjoy playing with animals …
a All the time
b Frequently
c Occasionally
d Never, they're too smelly.

7 You have …
a Endless patience, energy and lots of time
b A little patience, some energy, some time
c Little to no energy, very little patience and a very busy life
d A very short attention span and no energy

8 You have …
a A lot of common sense, you are responsible and never forget your duties
b Common sense, but you are quite busy and a little forgetful
c Too little time to do much, but can keep to a routine
d No sense of responsibility, you forget your duties and care only about yourself

Here are your scores

Mostly a's You have all or most of the qualities you need to be an excellent dog owner. Other suitable pets for you would be any large animals that require time, commitment and responsibility.

Mostly b's You should consider a smaller animal, such as a rabbit or a guinea pig. You love animals and are capable of caring for one well, but you just don't have the time or space for a larger animal.

Mostly c's A cat or fish would be perfect because although you love animals, you don't have the time or energy. A cat is perfect because although you would still need to feed and look after them they are fairly self-sufficient. Fish are also good because they don't need handling and they would be very relaxing to watch after a long day at the office.

Mostly d's Are you sure you really want a pet at all? Perhaps you could start off with a virtual pet, or Cyberpet, to see how you cope with the responsibility of owning a pet. Remember, real pets are animals, not toys and they need to be looked after, cared for and loved.

9 Interview with a vet

First copy the notes on a separate piece of paper. Then listen to the interview with veterinarian Dr Springer and take notes on what he says. In pairs, compare what you have written.

> Advantages
> Pets and children?
> Duties/disadvantages
> Effects on health
> Costs
> Exotic pets
> Problems with neighbours
> Other things to consider

10 Pet equipment

Unscramble the words and match them to the illustrations.

1 acchoprsstt
2 acehostu
3 beilorttx
4 aceg
5 aaimqruu
6 adel
7 deefgin wlbo
8 elmuzz
9 eegilnps abekst

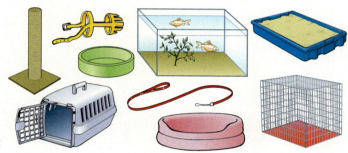

11 At the pet shop

Work with a partner to make a dialogue in English.

Customer

Sagen Sie, dass Sie in den nächsten Tagen einen Hund bekommen und Sie Zubehör kaufen möchten.

Sagen Sie, dass der Hund noch sehr klein ist und sie nicht genau wissen, wie groß er werden wird. Kaufen Sie einen kleinen Beißkorb und eine Leine und fragen Sie nach dem Preis eines Schlafkörbchens.

Sagen Sie, welchen Korb Sie möchten.

Sagen Sie, was Sie möchten.

Sagen Sie, dass Sie schon Bücher über Hunde zu Hause haben.

Shop assistant

Sagen Sie, dass man Leine und Beißkorb braucht, aber dass es viele verschiedene Größen gibt.

Zeigen Sie verschiedene Körbe und sagen Sie die Preise.

Bieten Sie Hundespielsachen und Hundefutter an.

Bieten Sie Bücher über Hunde an.

UNIT

11 | *Toys and games*

🎧 1 At the department store

Read the dialogue and answer the questions.

JOYCE Hello Peter, what are you doing here?
PETER Oh Joyce, what a surprise. I'm doing some Christmas shopping. I need a toy for my little nephew. It's quite difficult to find the right thing, isn't it?
JOYCE How old is he?
PETER He's seven. And the only things he seems to be interested in are guns and laser pistols and space invaders and things like that. It's awful, really, I don't want to buy war games, I really don't.
JOYCE Oh, well, they watch it all on television, don't they? And the toy industry is quite powerful. If they didn't do so much advertising no children would be interested in their monsters, I'm sure.
PETER I don't know much about toys, that's the problem. Daniel is just mad about technical toys and most of them seem awfully violent to me.
JOYCE But some of them are not quite as bad. Have you thought about a racing car set? They're fun. But I know what kids are like. My daughter drives me mad with all her doll's stuff. I've really tried hard not to let her slip into that mother-and-housewife role, but it seems I've got no chance.

1 Why does Peter find it difficult to get the right toy for Daniel?
2 Why does Joyce think children love certain toys so much?
3 Why is Joyce unhappy about her daughter playing with dolls?

77

2 In the toy department

Match the descriptions to the toys. Which toy do you think Peter should give his nephew?

WILD ADVENTURES™ OFF-ROADER helps children learn with Wild Adventures™ talking fact cards. 'Zebra'-Vehicle comes with explorer, pet toucan, video camera, water container and one talking fact card. Age 3 and up.

SING 'N COUNT SHEEP™. Buttons and colourful beads help baby learn to identify numbers and colours. Music, sounds and a twinkling light add to stimulating, learning fun. Requires 3 AA batteries (not included). Age 6 months and up.

3D PUZZLE. A combination of traditional puzzling and 3D modelling. Typical British and American tourist attractions, including Big Ben (120 pieces) and US Capitol Building (718 pieces). Age 12 years and up.

READING BEAR. Squeeze his foot and the reading bear reads your toddler one of 20 stories. The reading bear moves his head back and forth as he "reads" the open cloth book to his friend the mouse and your child. Soft-bodied. Age $1\frac{1}{2}$ and up.

GAME BOY™. Various exciting hand-held LCD games to keep your child entertained and trains eye/hand coordination. Sound on/off. Batteries supplied. Suitable for ages 8 and up.

DOLL'S HOUSE. Great for children on the move, this fully-furnished doll's house can be folded up for easy transport and storage. Dolls included. All parts in sturdy plastic. Age 4 and up.

LE MANS 24hr RACE SET. Complete with mains transformer. Includes two race cars with working headlights and magnetic base. 2 hand controllers. Track layout 137 x 72 cm. Running length 4-23m. Age 8 and up.

3 Any questions?

Read the descriptions above and find answers to the customers' questions.

1. Do I have to buy batteries for the LCD games or are they included?
2. Do we need a lot of space for the race set?
3. My niece is 4. Will the reading bear be a suitable present for her?
4. How many pieces are there in the 3D Big Ben puzzle?
5. What is included with the doll's house?
6. How many parts are there in the off-roader?
7. What can children do with the sing 'n count sheep?

4 Opposites

Find the words pairs with opposite meaning.

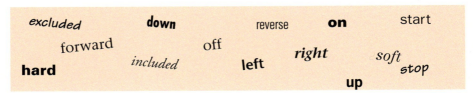

excluded   down   reverse   on   start
forward   off
included   left   right   soft
hard   up   stop

5 Working with words

Use words from exercise 4 to complete these sentences.

1. I'm sorry, batteries are not … but you can buy them in our hardware department.
2. You can turn the sound … and … by pressing this button.
3. Press the left button for … and the … one for reverse.
4. The doll house has also got a lift that goes … to the roof.
5. The doll's body is … – it's filled with synthetic material – but the head is … . I think it's made of plastic.
6. Take the escalator … to the basement.

6 Christmas shopping

SHOP ASSISTANT Can I help you?
PETER Yes, please. I'm looking for a present for my sister's son. I'm not sure what to buy. A friend of mine suggested a racing car set.
SHOP ASSISTANT Well, yes, if you'd like to have a look, I'll show you what we've got. How old is your nephew?
PETER He was seven last March. Do you think he's too young for that type of toy?
SHOP ASSISTANT No, I don't think so. He might need help at the start but they're very easy to operate. What about this one here, the Le Mans 24 hour? It costs £22.50. Or there's this one here, the Silverstone Speed. It's a quite a bit more expensive at £37.80.
PETER Oh dear.
SHOP ASSISTANT And here's another one for only £9.99.
PETER The prices vary a lot. What are the differences?
SHOP ASSISTANT This cheaper one here has a very short track and is very basic. The Le Mans has a longer track – it's 137 by 72 centimetres and the two racing cars have working headlights. And the Silverstone Speed …
PETER No, the Le Mans sounds good. I think he'd like that one.
SHOP ASSISTANT I'm sure he will. Is there anything else I can do for you?
PETER Do I need to buy batteries or are they included?
SHOP ASSISTANT No, it doesn't run on batteries. It comes with a mains transformer.
PETER Oh, that's fine. Just one more question – is it possible to return it? You know, just in case he doesn't like it or he's already got one.
SHOP ASSISTANT Yes, that's no problem. But you have to keep the original packaging and the receipt. Are you paying cash?
PETER I'd like to pay by credit card please, if that's possible.
SHOP ASSISTANT Yes of course, no problem.

Are the following sentences true or false? Correct the false statements.
1 Peter wants to buy a present for his nephew.
2 Peter's nephew is too young for a racing set.
3 Four racing cars are included in the Le Mans 24 hour set.
4 The set comes with batteries.
5 Peter cannot return the set if he loses the receipt.
6 The shop does not accept credit cards.

7 Dialogues

In pairs, act out dialogues selling toys. Use the descriptions in exercise 2 and the phrases in the dialogue in exercise 6 to help you.

8 The little shoplifter

Read the story and answer the questions.

It was a busy time at Nelson's department store, like every year just before Christmas. There were thousands of people pushing and shoving and it was quite difficult to get through the crowds. Joyce Robinson was in the middle of it all. 'Oh God,' she said to herself, 'I really don't know why this is called the most wonderful time of the year.' A young girl was standing next to her, waiting for the lift. 'Excuse me, do you know where the toys are?' Joyce asked the girl. 'Yes, they're on the second floor,' the girl said. 'Thank you, dear.' 'A nice girl,' Joyce thought, 'how old can she be? Eleven? Or twelve? She seems to be on her own.' As soon as the lift reached the second floor everyone got out.

Joyce went to buy some presents for her children, a doll's house, a detective game, a walking-talking monster and several other things. 'Do you want me to gift-wrap them?' the shop assistant asked her. 'No, thank you. I'll do that at home. If you could just give me a carrier bag, that'll do. Can I pay by credit card?' 'Yes, sure. Sign here please.'

Joyce was putting her biro back into her handbag when she saw the little girl she had met in the lift before. The girl was all in tears. 'What happened to you?' Joyce asked her. But the little girl did not answer. 'Do you know this girl?' the cashier asked Joyce. 'We caught her stealing a video game. Quite an expensive one. You know, normally we ring the police if we catch a shoplifter but this one is very young.' 'I only wanted to look at it,' said the little girl, still crying. 'But you put it in your pocket, young lady,' said the cashier.

'What are you going to do now? Will you ring her parents?' Joyce asked. 'No, please, don't ring my parents. I won't do it again. I promise! I promise!' Joyce felt sorry for the little thief, she was thinking of her own children and wondering if they would be so silly as to steal things. 'You know, that was a very stupid thing to do,' Joyce said to the girl. 'Can you see the sign here? Shoplifters will be prosecuted. Do you know what that means?' 'Will they put me in prison?' 'No, we won't put you in prison, but your parents may have to pay a fine if it's reported to the police,' the cashier said to the girl.

1. What do you think happened next?
2. What would you have done if you were the manager of the department?
3. What would you have done if you were Joyce Robinson?
4. Think of an ending to the story and discuss it in class.

> **GRAMMAR CHECK**
>
> **REPORTED SPEECH**
>
> *1* Shop assistant: 'How old **is** he?'
> She asked how old he **was**.
> *2* Peter: '**Can** I return it?'
> He asked whether/if he **could** return it.
> *3* Peter: 'I'**ll take** the Erupter.'
> Peter said he **would take** the Erupter.
>
> - *Steht das einleitende Verb in der Vergangenheit, verändern sich die Zeitform in der indirekten Rede ewa vom* simple present *zum* simple past *(1). Einige Hilfs- bzw. Modalverben verändern ihre Form:* can – could (2), will – would (3).

9 Practice

Rewrite the following sentences in reported speech.

1 John: 'How much is it?'
2 Anne: 'It's too expensive.'
3 Customer: 'I don't know much about toys.'
4 Shop assistant: 'I'll show you some teddy bears.'
5 Beth: 'Can you show me some toy cars?'
6 Peter: 'Can I pay by credit card?'
7 Susan: 'I'm sorry, we don't accept credit cards.'
8 I: 'We are sorry, the doll's house is out of stock.'
9 Joyce: 'Will you ring her parents?'

> **WORDS WITH MORE THAN ONE MEANING AND HOMONYMS**
>
> Some words have more than one meaning.
> I lost my door **key**.   There are black and white **keys** on the keyboard.
> Do you know the **key** to the exercise?
>
> Homonyms have different spelling and different meaning, but the same pronunciation.
> I'm very tired, I need a **break** now.   Use the **brake** to reduce the speed.
>
> Homonyms can also have the same spelling but different meanings and a different pronunciation.
> The baby doll has a pink **bow** in her hair.
> When you press the button, the elephants **bow** down.

10 Working with words

Here are eight German words which have more than one meaning. Find the correct English translations. How would you translate the remaining English words into German?

1. Bank (auf der man sitzt)   bank – bench
2. Tor (Tür)   goal – fool – gate
3. Blatt (am Baum)   sheet – leaf – paper
4. Decke (zum Zudecken)   blanket – table-cloth – ceiling
5. Absatz (eines Schuhs)   sales – paragraph – heel – landing
6. Karte (Speisekarte)   card – ticket – menu – map
7. Feder (eines Vogels)   spring – feather – nib
8. Rezept (vom Arzt)   prescription – recipe

11 Homonyms

Read the words in italics aloud and match them to a word in the brackets with a similar sound. Then translate the sentences into German.

1. Could you *read* the instructions please? (feed/bed)
2. I've *read* the instructions, but I don't understand them. (feed/bed)
3. The toy dog comes with a *lead* and a sleeping basket. (feed/bed)
4. Not many toys are made of *lead*. (feed/bed)
5. Be careful that you don't *tear* the paper. (here/hair)
6. When the baby doll is crying, there are even *tears* in her eyes. (here/hair)
7. Don't forget to *wind* the watch. (window/find)
8. Is there enough *wind* today for windsurfing? (window/find)

12 Puzzle

There are eleven words hidden in the puzzle which are pronounced the same as the words in the box but which are spelt differently. Find them and then translate the pairs of words into German.

H	W	P	E	S	T	E	E	L	O	O	R
S	E	L	I	T	H	T	I	A	W	I	P
R	S	A	F	O	M	A	U	B	A	T	I
A	R	I	R	E	W	O	L	F	S	M	E
E	T	N	A	B	O	T	H	U	T	L	C
B	A	O	R	T	L	F	T	H	E	R	E

bare ◆ fare ◆ flour
here ◆ peace ◆ plane
steal ◆ their ◆ two
waist ◆ weight

UNIT 12 | Dream job

🎧 1 Tom's job

Tom works in the children's department of a large shoe shop. A reporter from YOU magazine is interviewing him about his job.

YOU   So, Tom, how long have you worked here?
TOM   For nearly three years now.
YOU   And how did you get the job?
TOM   Through the job centre. This was the first interview they sent me on, and, luckily, the boss liked me.
YOU   What does the job involve?
TOM   Looking after the customers, measuring feet, and making sure that kids get the right fit. I don't work on the till though. A colleague does that.
YOU   What kind of qualities do you need to work here?
TOM   We get lots of tourists so it can be hard to communicate, especially as shoe sizes are different in other countries. I can speak a little French and a little German, which helps a lot.
YOU   And the hours?
TOM   I work from 11 am to 7 pm, with a lunch break of one hour. In fact, my break has just begun, so could you perhaps hurry up with the interview?
YOU   Yeah, no problem – just a few more questions. So, have you met any nice people through work?
TOM   Everyone knows everyone in here. Quite often a group of us go out together in the evening or at weekends.
YOU   And the pay?
TOM   Not too bad, it's above the minimum wage.
YOU   What's the best part of your job?
TOM   Working with such friendly staff.
YOU   And the worst?
TOM   Sweaty feet. Especially in summer.
YOU   Good point. And finally, what do you want to do in the future?
TOM   I'd like to be the shop manager, actually.

Compare the article in YOU magazine with the interview and correct the mistakes.

We've asked some people to tell us about their job. Working in retailing often means working on Saturdays, and last Saturday we caught up with Tom, 20, who works in the children's department of a large shoe shop. He got the job through an advert in the paper more than three years ago and since then he's been helping kids find the right shoes. Tom didn't need any special training for the job but quite often foreign customers come to his shop, so it's great that he's got basic knowledge of Spanish and German. He usually works 8 hours a day and he says the pay is OK, but unfortunately he doesn't get on with his colleagues very well. His plans for the future? One day he'd like to run a shop.

2 Valerie's job

Valerie is a sales assistant at an Internet café and mobile phone stall. She was asked the same questions as Tom. In pairs, use her answers to make up an interview like the one in exercise 1.

- 9.30 to 4.30.
- The money.
- It's really good for my age and I get discounts as well.
- Helping customers to use the computers or buy the right mobile phone or accessories.
- Well, you need good knowledge of the products we sell and you have to be familiar with the Internet.
- Since last summer.
- Yes, quite a few.
- I heard they needed someone so I phoned. I did a trial period and was offered a job.
- Travelling to work takes ages, which makes the day a drag.
- I'd like to work nearer to where I live. That will be a priority with my next job.

3 Working with words

Find the suitable definitions on the right for the words on the left.

1	colleague	work longer than regular working hours
2	job centre	work in the morning, evening or night
3	day off	time where you stop working, for example to have lunch
4	staff	reduction on prices
5	wage	give work to someone
6	employee	pay you get monthly, usually for work in shops or offices
7	work overtime	pay you get weekly, usually for manual work
8	employers	people or companies who employ others
9	employ	a day when you don't have to work
10	break	person who works for someone in return for wages or salary
11	discount	person who works with you in the same place
12	work in shifts	all people who work in the same place
13	salary	office that gives information about available jobs

4 What about you?

In pairs, interview each other about the jobs that you have had.

> **GRAMMAR CHECK**
>
> **SIMPLE PAST AND PRESENT PERFECT (CONTINUOUS)**
>
> 1 Tom **started** to work there more than three years ago.
> 2 How long **have** you **worked** here?
> 3 My break **has** just **begun** so could you hurry up with the interview?
> 4 Since then he**'s** (= **has**) **been helping** kids find the right shoes.
>
> - *Im* simple past *wird ein in der Vergangenheit vollständig abgeschlossener Vorgang geschildert (1). Es wird häufig mit einer Zeitangabe der Vergangenheit* (yesterday, last week, three years ago, *usw.) verwendet.*
> - *Das* present perfect *dagegen drückt aus, dass ein Zustand oder eine Handlung in der Vergangenheit begonnen hat und noch immer andauert (2) bzw. noch Auswirkung auf die Gegenwart hat (3). Signalwörter sind u. a.* since, for, already, yet, just, ever *und* never.
> - *Bei der Verlaufsform des* present perfect (present perfect continuous) *wird die Dauer der Verhandlung hervorgehoben (4).*

5 Practice

Find the correct form of the words in brackets. Be careful with the word order.

1 I … (always/want) to become a shop assistant.
2 I … (hear) from a friend that the position is vacant.
3 He … (get) a rise last month.
4 … (you/ever/try) to find a job nearer to where you live?
5 The personnel manager … (talk) to me yesterday.
6 I … (never/work) in shifts before.
7 I … (not/have) a day off last week.
8 She … (just/arrive) at her place of work.
9 … (she/have) the job interview yet?
10 The personnel manager … (not/see) her yet.
11 How long … (you/work) here?
12 How much … (you/earn) when you … (work) in the shoe shop?

6 Practice

Write the present perfect continuous forms of the verbs in brackets and translate the sentences into German.

1. He … (try) to repair the machine all afternoon.
2. What … (you/do) all afternoon?
3. I … (think) about it.
4. She … (sell) shoes for many years.
5. He … (work) overtime everyday for months.
6. I … (run) around all day.
7. … (they/make) good profits this year?
8. They … (use) this product for years.

GRAMMAR CHECK

SINCE/FOR/AGO

1. I've been here **since** Monday.
2. She's lived here **for** 20 years.
3. They closed down their shop two weeks **ago**.

Since *(seit)* bezeichnet den Zeitpunkt, an dem die Handlung begonnen hat *(1)*.
For *(seit)* drückt die Dauer der Handlung aus *(2)*.
Ago *(vor)* bezeichnet einen zurückliegenden Zeitraum *(3)*.

- *Beachten Sie: Um auszudrücken, dass ein Vorgang in der Gegenwart noch andauert, gebraucht man im Englischen das present perfect, im Deutschen dagegen die Gegenwart.*

7 Practice

Complete the sentences with *since*, *for* or *ago*.

1. I've lived in this city … I was born.
2. The goods arrived a few minutes … .
3. They've been waiting … three o'clock.
4. She's been selling fabrics … a couple of years.
5. They've been at this company … 1990.
6. I've been with this company … a long time.
7. She's been learning French … two years.
8. She left school some time … .
9. We've been working here … years.
10. They promised me a rise three weeks … .
11. They've had their shop at High Gate … 1997.
12. They moved to High Gate some years … .

8 Situations vacant

SUPERMARKET
needs part-time shop assistant for the deli counter. 20 hours/5 day week, good working conditions.
Phone 568 9394

Barnes Home and Furnishing

Our business is expanding and we are looking for young, ambitious people to sell furniture and home textiles in our new shop in High Gate. If you have experience in selling, phone Ms Campbell on 678 6371

Do you speak a foreign language?

Fashion boutique in large city hotel needs full-time shop assistant. You should speak French or German fluently, basic knowledge of other foreign languages an advantage. Good pay.

Send your curriculum vitae to
Boutique MaBelle, Intercity Hotel, 102 Park Lane, London WC1.

Look at the three adverts and find the English expression for the following words

1. Bezahlung
2. ehrgeizig
3. Erfahrung
4. Vorteil
5. ganztags
6. Geschäft
7. fließend
8. Teilzeit
9. Grundkenntnisse
10. Lebenslauf
11. vergrößern
12. Arbeitsbedingungen

9 Getting a job

Hannah Cassidy is interested in the job at Barnes. Listen to the telephone conversation and complete her notes.

Job at Barnes still vacant!
They sell furniture, ...1, china and ...2.
Hours: ...3 to ...4, Saturdays (only every ...5) until ...6
Pay: ...7
Interview with staff manager - Mr ...8
When: ...9 at 2 pm.
Where: in the High Gate shopping centre, ...10 floor

10 A job interview

Carol Robinson is interested in the position as a part-time shop assistant at the deli counter. Complete the job interview with the correct forms of the words in brackets. Take care with the word order. Listen to the CD to check your answers.

INTERVIEWER When …1 (you/be) born, Ms Robinson?
CAROL I …2 (be) born in 1970.
INTERVIEWER And …3 (you/always/live) in this city?
CAROL No, I …4 (live) in the country when I was a child.
INTERVIEWER …5 (you/ever/work) as a shop assistant before?
CAROL Yes, I …6 (work) in a department store for 8 years, but I …7 (leave) after my daughter Jessica … 8 (be) born.
INTERVIEWER When …9 (be) that?
CAROL 6 years ago.
INTERVIEWER And …10 (you/not have) a job since then?
CAROL Well, I …11 (work) as a part-time cashier in a supermarket, but only for four months. That …12 (be) last year. But it …13 (become) too much for me, the stress, you know. But Jessica …14 (start) school last September and so I'm trying to find a job again.

11 Puzzle

Find the English translation of the following words in the puzzle below. Then write a paragraph or two about your own job using these words.

1 Arbeitgeber
2 Arbeitnehmer
3 Arbeitszeit
4 Belegschaft
5 Chef
6 freier Tag
7 Gehalt
8 Gehaltserhöhung
9 Kollege/Kollegin
10 Pause
11 Schicht
12 Überstunden
13 Urlaub

S	R	U	O	H	G	N	I	K	R	O	W
R	H	F	F	O	Y	A	D	I	Z	Y	A
E	Y	I	K	T	V	X	S	Z	H	R	J
Y	Y	M	F	V	R	E	G	A	N	A	M
O	E	Y	V	T	L	H	R	Q	M	L	I
L	Y	A	D	I	L	O	H	T	A	A	Z
P	E	E	Y	O	L	P	M	E	I	S	X
M	C	O	L	L	E	A	G	U	E	M	H
E	B	R	E	A	K	S	T	A	F	F	E

12 Hannah's new job?

In pairs, act out the interview between Hannah and Mr Blackwell, the staff manager at Barnes. Student A (Hannah) look at File 9 on page 100.

Student B (Mr Blackwell) ask 'Hannah' questions to find as much information as possible to fill in the form. Take notes on a separate piece of paper.

1 name
2 place and date of birth
3 education
4 present job
5 other job experience
6 reason for leaving present job
7 special abilities
8 foreign languages
9 other

ALL / NONE / BOTH / EITHER / NEITHER

all (of many)	We interviewed five applicants. **All** (of them) were suitable.
none (of many)	**None** of them was/were late for the interview.
both (of two)	We have two main stores. **Both** (of them) need new staff.
neither (of two)	**Neither** (store/of them) has a toy department.
either (one of two)	Hannah said she could work in **either** store.
both … and	**Both** Hannah **and** Tania want full-time jobs.
neither … nor	**Neither** Adam **nor** Rochelle wants to work in the furniture department.
either … or	**Either** Tania **or** Hannah would be best for the job.

13 Practice

After his interview with Hannah, Mr Blackwell discusses the applicants with a colleague. Complete the sentences with words from the box.

> either ◆ neither ◆ both ◆ or ◆ nor ◆ and ◆ all ◆ none

1 "Well, we had a lot of applicants and they … seem very good."
2 "… Adam … Tania can work on Saturdays, which is too bad."
3 "… of them can start next week because they … have other jobs."
4 "… Hannah … Rochelle have experience in fabrics."
5 "We could … put Tania in the tableware … the china section."
6 "She said she would be happy to work in … department."
7 "I like … Adam … Jill, but … of them has experience in selling furniture."
8 "Perhaps we could give … of them a job."

Business correspondence

1 Parts of a business letter

Work with a partner to label the parts (1–12) of the letter with words from the box. If you're not sure of an answer, ask another pair.

> (carbon) copies ◆ body of the letter ◆ complimentary close
> date ◆ enclosures ◆ inside address ◆ letterhead ◆ paragraph
> reference ◆ salutation ◆ signature ◆ subject line

1 — **Barnes Home and Furnishing**

44 HIGH GATE LONDON NW67PB
email: barnes@home.co.uk

2 — Ref. AM/PC
3 — 6 Feb 20..

Ms Margery Quant
7 Ivinghoe Close
Harrow
Middx HA6 3XO — 4

5 — Dear Ms Quant

6 — **Your order dated 17 January**

Thank you very much for your order of tableware. The milk jug (ref. no. 34978) and the sugar bowl (ref. no. 34076) have been sent to you.

However, we are very sorry to inform you that the dinner plates (ref. no. 34978) as well as the sets of cups and saucers (ref. no. 34486) from our Celtic Blue collection are out of stock at the moment. We expect to receive the goods within the next five weeks and will inform you of the date of delivery as soon as possible.

8 —

— 7

We would like to apologize for the delay and thank you once again for your interest in our products.

9 — Yours sincerely

10 — *Angus McIntosh*
Angus McIntosh

11 — cc A. Clarke
12 — Enc New Catalogue

2 How to write a business letter

Work with a partner to see how much you know about business letters. Compare your answers with another pair.

1. Whose initials are often stated in references?
2. Why should you not write a date this way: 5/7/02
3. When you are answering a letter, what should you be careful about?
4. Which of these salutations should be used to address a man, an unmarried woman, a married woman?
   a Miss   b Mrs   c Ms   d Mr
5. Where do you write the subject line in an English business letter?
6. Where do you leave a line space?
7. Find the matching complimentary close for these salutations.
   a Dear Ms Jordan   Yours faithfully
   b Dear William   Yours sincerely
   c Dear Sir or Madam   With best regards
8. How do you show a) that you've put something else in the envelope and b) that you've sent a copy of the letter to someone else?

3 An invoice

Look at the invoice below and find the abbreviations or the symbols for the following expressions. Find out their meaning. You may use a dictionary for help.

public limited company ◆ and ◆ company ◆ delivery ◆ for the attention of ◆ Gardens ◆ limited company ◆ Middlesex ◆ October ◆ per cent ◆ reference ◆ value added tax

Springfield & Co Potteries Ltd.
43–45 Bouverie Gdns
Kenton Harrow
Middx HA3 ORQ

Barnes Furnishing Store plc
attn Ms A Clarke
44 High Gate
London NW6 7PB

Date: 5 Oct 20..

INVOICE

description	ref number	quantity	item price	total price
sugar bowl	34076	5	4.38	21.75
milk jug	64398	5	4.48	22.40
dinner plates	34958	40	3.76	150.38
cups and saucers	34486	40	3.66	146.26
			SUB-TOTAL	£340.79
			+ VAT	£59.64
			TOTAL	£400.43

Terms: 5 % if paid within 10 days, 30 days net.
Del. 5 weeks

4 A complaint

Copy the letter and complete it with the words below.

> cc/F Norman ◆ Enc ◆ A Clarke (Ms)
> Dear Sir or Madam ◆ delivered
> Our Order No 582 of 2 September 20..
> 43-45 Bouverie Gdns ◆ incomplete
> Yours faithfully ◆ invoice ◆ missing
> Ref: AC/EK

Barnes Home and Furnishing

44 HIGH GATE LONDON NW67PB
email: barnes@home.co.uk

...1
Date: 8 October 20..

Springfield & Co Potteries Ltd
...2
Kenton
Harrow
Middx HA3 ORQ

...3

...4

The above order of Celtic Blue china tableware has just been ...5 to our warehouse.

When we checked the consignment against our order we found out that it was ...6. Instead of the 5 milk jugs, ref. no. 34398, ordered, you had only sent us 3.

Perhaps you could look into the matter and send us the ...7 milk jugs as soon as possible. We will send you the incorrect ...8 by mail and we are looking forward to receiving your reply very soon.

...9

...10

...11

...12

5 Reply to a complaint

Scott Brown has just left school and now works as an assistant to Ms Potter at Springfield & Co. One morning he finds a message from his boss on his voicemail. Listen to the message and help Scott write the e-mail reply to the letter in exercise 4.

6 Puzzle

Find the full words for the following abbreviations in the puzzle. Write them down on a separate piece of paper.

D	E	T	A	R	O	P	R	O	C	N	I
Y	R	O	A	D	S	T	R	E	E	T	E
Y	L	I	M	I	T	E	D	O	U	A	O
P	E	U	L	A	V	A	D	D	E	D	O
O	C	E	E	N	C	L	O	S	U	R	E
C	E	U	N	E	V	A	T	A	X	U	H
C	A	R	B	O	N	P	U	B	L	I	C
Y	N	A	P	M	O	C	V	B	P	N	K

cc ♦ Inc ♦ plc
VAT ♦ enc ♦ RD
ST ♦ Ave ♦ Co

7 A virtual shop

Read the shopping guide of a virtual shop in the Internet and answer the customers' FAQs (frequently asked questions).

1 How do you get to different parts of the shop?
2 How can you find out if a certain article, eg a CD, is available?
3 How do you know the price of the article?
4 What do you do once you have found an article you want to buy?
5 What should you do if you change your mind and don't want to buy the article that's already in your cart?
6 How can you see which articles are in your shopping cart?
7 How is the order finalized?
8 How do you pay?
9 What about safety of payment?

 Add to basket   Delivery

Moving through the store

If you want to look for an item in a particular part of our store, just click one of the tabs at the top of the page.

BROWSE

You can simply select a category that interests you, click on it, and explore the listings in that area.

Details

If you click on the name of a particular product, you'll get more detailed information like:

* picture of the product
* description
* price
* availability

SEARCH

Type the keywords in the search box and click 'go'. We'll give you a list of all products that match your search words.

[   ] GO!

Add an item to your shopping cart

When you have found an item you would like to buy, simply click on the **Add to Shopping Cart** button. Just like in a physical store, your Shopping Cart holds the items until you are ready to check out. From the Shopping Cart you can:
* Proceed to checkout
* Keep shopping
* Delete or save items for later

You can always get back to your cart by clicking the shopping cart icon found at the top of the page.

CHECK OUT

We'll walk you through the steps necessary to complete your order, and give you the opportunity to choose from a variety of shipping and gift-wrapping options.

Don't worry, you haven't finalized your order till you click the **Place Your Order** button that appears at the very end of the purchase process. Also, we never charge your credit card until your order ships.

SAFE PAYMENT

We guarantee that every transaction you make will be 100% safe. This means you pay nothing if unauthorized charges are made to your credit card as a result of shopping at our company. You still don't want to use your credit card number on the Internet? No problem. Enter only your card's last five digits and its expiry date. Once you have fully submitted your order, you will be prompted with a phone number that you can use to call in the rest of your card number.

Pairwork files

File 1, Unit 2, Exercise 12

Student B: You take orders over the telephone for a sports shop. Use the information below to take your caller's order. Remember, many of the items are sold out so you might have to offer the caller a second choice.

Hooded sweat cardigan with two front pockets, long sleeves and a drawcord fastening. Washable. Cotton. Grey, black or green Men's sizes S, M, L, XL. ~~€75.00~~ €30.00

Tracksuit bottoms with elasticated drawcord waist and tape detail down the side of the leg. Washable. Polyester. Brown. YX 1381 ~~S~~, M, ~~L~~, XL ~~€34.00~~ €25.00

Cotton jersey leggings. Lycra for a perfect fit. Ankle length. Washable. 80% cotton, 15% polyester, 5% Lycra. Navy, black or grey.
~~Short fitting sizes (inside leg 27 ins) S, M, L, XL €18.50.~~
Standard fitting sizes (inside leg 29 ins) S, ~~M~~, ~~L~~, XL €19.50.

Tank top. Washable. 95% cotton, 5% Lycra. Blue, chocolate or ~~red~~. Sizes S, M, L, XL €10.50

Chocolate no longer available in sizes L, XL; blue only available in S

Fleece top with two side pockets and embroidered logo. Polyester polar fleece. Lilac, ~~cherry~~ or lemon. Sizes S, M, L, XL €68.00

lemon available in all sizes, lilac in all sizes except S and L

Tracksuit. Top with front zip fastening and two side pockets. Bottoms with elasticated waist. Tape detail. 100% polyester. Lilac, green. Sizes S, M, L, XL €53.50

Lilac available in S, M only; Green available in XL only

File 2, Unit 8, Exercise 9

Annie / Andy

You have been a strict vegetarian for ten years. You think it is disgusting to eat the flesh of other animals. You feel sorry for all animals that are raised just to be eaten. What kind of life can that be? You believe that you do not need to eat meat if you want to have a balanced diet because you can get everything you need (like protein) from non-meat products.

File 3, Unit 6, Exercise 9

STUDENT B: Your partner has the instructions on how to use the video recorder. Ask him/her for the missing information and complete the text below.

START LIKE THIS   Which button do I press to turn the video recorder on? How do I start ... ?

If you want to see a video, you have to switch on the video recorder first. Press the   1   button and insert the tape. Make sure that the television set is on and then press the   2   button to play the video tape. If you want to stop the tape at a certain point you can either press the   3   button, then the tape comes to a full stop, or you can press the   4   button and you can see a still picture. If you press the   5   button in this position you can see the video at high speed without sound and if you press the   6   button you can see playback picture at high speed. You will need that when you are looking for a certain section in a film. You can mark a certain point in the film by putting the tape counter to zero. To do that, you have to check first that the tape counter is on. If you press the   7   button you can switch between the current time and the tape counter. Then you press the   8   button to put the counter to zero. If you want to wind the tape forward, press the   9   button. When you have finished watching the film, rewind the tape by pressing the   10   button and wait till the tape comes to a stop. Again press the   11   button to switch the video recorder off.

File 4, Unit 8, Exercise 9

Bob / Barbara

You like animals, but you think it is natural for humans to eat them. You believe that meat is a necessary part of a balanced diet and that people will not get enough protein if they don't eat any meat at all. But last week you watched a TV programme about battery chickens and it was horrible how they kept the animals in small cages. You think there should be stricter laws to make sure that animals used for food have enough space to live in and are not treated cruelly. It might cost more but it's worth it.

File 5, Unit 5, Exercise 2

Dictate the following names and addresses to your partner.

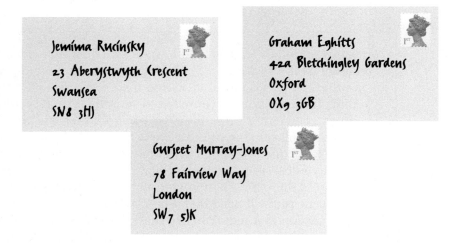

File 6, Unit 8, Exercise 9

Charla / Charles

You are not a vegetarian and you think that vegetarians who eat eggs are being hypocritical – if they care so much about animals, how can they eat eggs from chickens kept in such cruel conditions? You think that stricter rules in Britain about the way animals are kept would make British products too expensive for people to buy. Instead of spending more on free-range chicken or organically produced food, people would just buy cheaper imported products produced in the old, cruel way.

File 7, Unit 9, Exercise 7

THROUGHOUT HISTORY, gemstones have been said to have certain energies and healing qualities. Whether you believe in their secret powers or not, the simple beauty of precious and semi-precious stones makes them an elegant accessory for men and women. Here is a little guide to some of the most common stones.

- *Opal* enhances creativity, love, happiness and joy and intensifies sexual attraction. The stone helps its bearer to use logic when solving disputes. (photo 12)

- *Rock Crystal* is a transparent stone primarily used for foretelling the future. Crystal balls are made from it. It brings luck as well spiritual and mental calm. (photo 9)

- *Ruby* is a very powerful stone and has a great deal of energy. It creates in its bearer a feeling of inner power. It is considered to clear and purify negative thoughts. (photo 1)

- *Sapphire* comes in many colours, ranging from yellow to black. It enhances the inner wisdom of a person and suppresses negative emotions such as jealousy and envy. (photo 11)

- *Topaz* increases physical energy and vitality and is good for eating problems. It improves the appetite and the sense of taste and is also good for those who wish to lose weight. (photo 6)

- *Turquoise* is considered to bring great luck to its bearer. It is known as a stone that wards off disasters. When it is given as a gift it brings a special blessing to the recipient. (photo 8)

File 8, Unit 8, Exercise 9

Denise / Dennis

You are not a strict vegetarian, but you avoid eating meat whenever you can. When it is awkward to avoid eating meat (for example when you are invited out to a restaurant or when you are eating at a friend's house), then you will eat it – no problem. But you feel healthier when you don't eat meat and you enjoy eating other kinds of food. Perhaps it's a good idea to make animal products more expensive. Then people might eat less of them and they would be healthier.

File 9, Unit 12, Exercise 12

Student A: You are Hannah. Use the information below to answer the staff manager's questions.

Hannah Anne Cassidy was born on 4 February 1982 in London. She attended Primary and Secondary School in Clapham, London. After school she started as a trainee shop assistant at Richards & Co in Princess Square. She has been with this company since 1 August 1998 but they are closing so she needs to find a new job. She hopes to find a job nearer to her home as the other company was so far away and she had to travel more than an hour and a half everyday to get there. She could start the new job in 6 weeks. She has a lot of experience in dealing with customers and a good knowledge of fabrics. Hannah is familiar with working on computers but she cannot type very well. She has basic knowledge of French and she has a driving licence but doesn't yet have a car.

File 10, Unit 4, Exercise 9

Student B: Look at the plan of Patricia's room below. Try to find as many differences as you can between your plan and Student A's plan.

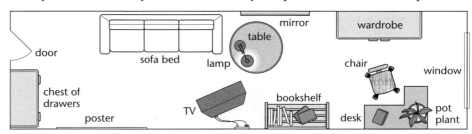

Transcripts

Unit 1 Exercise 6

PATRICIA   I'd like to try on the beige shoes with the strap you've got in your shop window.
ASSISTANT   Certainly, madam. Which ones exactly do you mean?
PATRICIA   The beige ones on the top shelf, the ones with the medium heel.
ASSISTANT   Oh, yes. What's your size?
PATRICIA   Size $6\frac{1}{2}$, please.
ASSISTANT   Just one moment please. I'll get them. Please take a seat.
PATRICIA   Thank you.
ASSISTANT   I'm sorry madam, we've only got size 6 left. Would you like to try them on?
PATRICIA   Well, I'll try. … No, I'm afraid they are too tight here at the toes. I'm sure they'll hurt when I walk around.
ASSISTANT   That's too bad. I'm afraid I haven't got a bigger pair. But we've got another branch in Orchard Street, that's not far from here. If you like, I could ring and ask if they have got a size $6\frac{1}{2}$.
PATRICIA   A branch in Orchard Street? Oh yes, I know where it is. It's on my way anyway. I can go there right now, if there's time enough. What time do they close?
ASSISTANT   All our shops are open until 7 pm, it's only a quarter past 6 now. If you go there straight away there's plenty of time. But if you just wait a minute, I'll ring them up first.
PATRICIA   Thank you very much, that's very kind.

Unit 2 Exercise 6

Boost blood flow to the brain with this easy yoga move.

HOW TO DO IT
Stand erect with arms outstretched, palms down.
Arms should be in line with shoulders.
Picture a clock on the floor, under your feet face up.
Then begin to spin, turning in a clockwise direction.
Begin and end slowly, building up speed and deceleration gradually.
Focus your vision on a single point ahead of you to prevent you from getting too dizzy.

HOW IT WORKS
Spinning enhances circulation, which in turn increases the energy flow through the top of the head. It also aids the flow of spinal fluid, which contributes to mental clarity.

Unit 2 Exercise 8

DJ   *Dr Runner, can you tell our listeners why it is so important to do regular exercise?*

RR   If you are physically inactive, you may have a higher risk of coronary heart disease. But physical inactivity is just one of many risk factors involved. These factors also include diabetes, cigarette smoking, high cholesterol and extreme overweight. Regular exercise strengthens your heart and lungs and makes them work better. When you exercise regularly, you burn calories. Exercise also builds and strengthens bones, joints and muscles. It prevents high blood pressure and lowers the cholesterol level.

DJ   *Are there any risks involved in exercising?*

RR   Well, if done properly and sensibly, exercise should be a safe and pleasant experience. You should consult a doctor if you have chest pain, joint or bone problems or if you become breathless easily.

DJ   *Which exercises should I do?*

RR   Pick activities you enjoy. You are more likely to stay with your exercise programme if you do something you like. Very good for your heart and lungs, for example, are the following activities: brisk walking, aerobics, dancing, cycling, cross-country skiing, hiking, skating, jogging, swimming, and tennis.

DJ   *Do I need to be specially equipped or dressed to exercise?*

RR   As you can see from the suggested list of sports and exercises, many activities do not require special equipment or clothing. You should dress appropriately for the activity and weather. Choose loose-fitting, comfortable clothes and shoes. Do not use rubberized, nonporous material.

DJ   *One last piece of advice you would like to give us?*

RR   Remember to drink plenty of fluids before, during and after exercise.

DJ   *That was highly interesting. Thank you very much for the interview, Doctor Runner. And now let's take some callers.*

Unit 3 Exercise 2

YASMINA ILGAR   I do some sewing from time to time and I love working with fabrics like painting on silk. I enjoy designing my own clothes and sometimes I succeed in creating something really special. I am planning to attend an evening course on fashion design next September.

KIM BENNET   I take evening classes in Italian. When I was a child I went to Italy with my parents several times, and I learned to speak the language a little. When I was in Florence last summer I noticed I was quite good at understanding the language. But I had great problems with speaking and grammar and so I started going to evening classes. Since I started work I've had very little time but I try to study as often as I can. I would like to live in Italy for some time and I'll try to find a job there.

BRIAN RUSSELL   I am quite interested in hiking and mountain climbing. My parents are very keen on hiking but when I was a child I hated it and I refused to go with them. I preferred watching

	TV or playing with my friends. But now my friends and I enjoy exploring the countryside, and sleeping in tents gives us a thrilling feeling of adventure. We are looking forward to spending our summer holiday in the Alps.
PAMELA TAYLOR	I like to do some exercise after work, so I've become a member of a fitness centre. Many of them are very expensive but I've found one that offers reductions for young people and I can afford to go there twice a week. In summer when the weather is fine I enjoy outdoor activities, so I do some swimming or cycling. But in winter when it gets dark so early I prefer exercising indoors.
DENNIS LITTLEWOOD	My hobby is playing football. I've been a member of our local football club since I was a little boy. We train three times a week and on Sundays we often have matches. So I have little time for other things. But all my friends are there and so I really enjoy it. For years we've just missed out on being top of the league, but last year we finally succeeded in winning most of our matches and we managed to win the league.

Unit 4 Exercise 1

SALLY	Hello?
PATRICIA	Hello, this is Patricia Taylor. I've just seen your ad in the paper and I'm calling about the room. Is it still available?
SALLY	Yes, you're the third caller but nobody's taken it yet. Shall I tell you something about our place?
PATRICIA	Yes please.
SALLY	Well, there're four bedrooms all together and the lounge – you'd have to share that with the other people here, and there's a kitchen and a bathroom.
PATRICIA	Is it a house or a flat?
SALLY	It's a semi-detached house, we've also got a little garden at the back.
PATRICIA	Oh really? That's lovely. What about heating?
SALLY	There's gas central heating. And we've also got a washing-machine and a tumble-dryer that you could use.
PATRICIA	Could you tell me something about the other people who live there?
SALLY	I'm a secretary, oh, I haven't even told you my name, I'm sorry. I'm Sally King. David works for a computer company and Sheila, she's David's girlfriend, is a nurse. And then there's Harald. He is a law student from Austria. They're all very nice.
PATRICIA	Well, it sounds great. I'm really interested. By the way, how much is the deposit?
SALLY	It's £200. Would you like to come and see us?
PATRICIA	Yes, I'd love to. When would it be all right with you?
SALLY	What about this evening at about 7? I'm not sure about Sheila's working hours but the others should be at home so you could meet us then.
PATRICIA	Oh yes, I could make that.
SALLY	Do you know how to get here? It's …

Unit 5 Exercise 1

RECEPTIONIST	Barnes Home and Furnishing. Good morning.
MAN	I'd like to speak to Alan Macintosh, please.
RECEPTIONIST	Sorry, he's not in at the moment. Can I take a message?
MAN	Could you tell him to ring me back please? My name is Abdul El-Rashidi.
RECEPTIONIST	Could you spell your name please?
MAN	Sure, that's A-B-D-U-L E-L hyphen R-A-S-H-I-D-I, and my number is 128 7359.
RECEPTIONIST	128 7359.
MAN	That's right.
RECEPTIONIST	OK, Mr El-Rashidi. I'll tell Mr Macintosh as soon as he's back.

Unit 5 Exercise 3

RECEPTIONIST	Barnes Home and Furnishing. Hello?
MS QUANT	Hello, I'd like to order some tableware.
RECEPTIONIST	Yes, hold on a minute, I'll connect you to our china and crockery department.
ALAN	China and crockery department, Alan Macintosh.
MS QUANT	Hello, my name's Margery Quant. I'd like to order some items from your Summertime collection if that's possible.
ALAN	Yes, of course. That's no problem. Do you happen to know the reference numbers?
MS QUANT	Yes, I've got the catalogue right here.
ALAN	If you'd just hold on a second, I'll get a pen…Yes?
MS QUANT	That's two dessert plates, diameter 22cm, reference number 43643G, item price £4, one milk jug, reference number 43123V, item price £8, and three mugs, reference number 43381X item price £3.50.
ALAN	Yes, I've got that. Anything else?
MS QUANT	And two of my cups are broken – can I buy cups without saucers?
ALAN	No, I'm sorry, they come as a set, you see.
MS QUANT	All right, make it two cups and saucers, then. The reference number is 43876Q, item price £5.
ALAN	Anything else?
MS QUANT	No, thank you, that's all.
ALAN	That's two dessert plates, one milk jug, three mugs and two cups and saucers. Have you got a customer number?
MS QUANT	No, I haven't.
ALAN	OK. Could you give me your name and address, please?
MS QUANT	My name is Margery Quant, and I live in 7, Ivinghoe Close …
ALAN	One moment. Could you spell your name please?
MS QUANT	M-A-R-G-E-R-Y Q-U-A-N-T.
ALAN	Q-U-A-N-T. OK, I've got that. And the address?
MS QUANT	Number 7, Ivinghoe Close. That's I-V-I-N-G-H-O-E C-L-O-S-E. Harrow, Middlesex, the postcode is HA6 3XO.
ALAN	HA6 3XO. Could you give me your telephone number just in case we need to contact you?

MS QUANT   It's 0208 475 9754. Do you charge for delivery?
ALAN   Yes, it'll be £3 because the total amount is under £100. Otherwise it would be free.
MS QUANT   I see. Yes, that's fine. How do I pay?
ALAN   You can give me your credit card number or you can pay cash on delivery.
MS QUANT   I'll pay cash on delivery, if that's all right.
ALAN   Yes, of course.
MS QUANT   And how long will it take?
ALAN   If everything's in stock, which I think it is, you'll have the goods within three or four days. If not we will have to order them but it won't take more than 10 days or so. Would that be all right?
MS QUANT   Yes, that's fine. Thanks a lot. Bye, bye.
ALAN   Good bye, Ms Quant.

Unit 5 Exercise 12

What you do

1 Cut sponge cake into 2 cm cubes and place in serving dish. Drizzle sherry over the cake.

2 Pour boiling water over jelly crystals and stir until dissolved. Add cold water. Pour into a large tin and refrigerate until set.

3 Prepare the custard according to the instructions on the packet. Remove from heat, add the egg and mix well. Cover surface with plastic wrap, cool to room temperature.

4 Cut jelly into cubes. Place in a layer on top of the sponge. Add fruit for the next layer, then pour custard over top. Refrigerate for at least 20 minutes.

5 Whip cream with icing sugar and put decoratively onto trifle and garnish with strawberries.

Unit 7 Exercise 7

Ingredients
1 beaten egg
½ teaspoon olive oil
1 tablespoon flour
½ teaspoon sea salt
1 tablespoon whole milk

Mix all ingredients until they are thoroughly blended. Spread the mixture over your face and neck and leave it on for about 15 minutes. Rinse well with cool water and pat dry.

Unit 9 Exercise 9

Natalie Thompson
I was preparing supper in the kitchen. Suddenly I heard a strange noise outside. It was so loud that the baby woke up and started crying.

Charles McGyre
I was watching my favourite programme on the telly. There was an alarm going off somewhere, so I could hardly hear what was happening on television.

Sharon Graham
I was going upstairs to close the curtains in my bedroom when I heard something. Normally my husband draws the curtains, but he was feeding the cats. I looked out of the window, but I didn't see anything unusual.

Nancy Jones
I was phoning my sister. I was just telling her about my new job. Then I heard a scream.

Alistair O'Neil
I was standing at my front door looking for the key when I saw something happening at the jewellery shop up the street.

George Shepherd
I was taking the dog for a walk, and then suddenly a blue car drove past me and stopped in front of Steve Wellington's jewellery shop. I heard a strange noise inside and at the same time a light went on. Someone screamed and then the alarm sounded. Suddenly two men ran out of the shop.

Unit 10 Exercise 3

1 I need a machine to cut the grass. What is it called in English?
2 My sister is moving into her new flat and she needs things like … you know … hammers and screwdrivers. Do you have a … er … box with all these things in it?

3 My brother's birthday is next week and he likes making things like tables and shelves and things like that. I want to give him an electric machine you use to cut wood. What's it called in English?
4 Help me, please. My dog is so wild – she never listens to me. She sees a cat and ... whoosh ... she's gone. I need something so she can't run away when we go walking. I don't know what the thing is called.
It is like a rope. Can you help?
5 I've just moved into a house with a garden. And now I would like to cook meals outside like the English sometimes do. Do you have a ... what do you call it? A cooker for the garden?

Unit 10 Exercise 7

INTERVIEWER   What are the advantages of living with a pet?
DR SPRINGER   If you have ever had a pet, you will know how much love and happiness they can bring to your home. Pets bring a little bit of nature back to your home, especially if you live in a city. Pets are wonderful companions for anyone who sometimes feels lonely.
INTERVIEWER   Why is it good for a child to have a pet?
DR SPRINGER   When caring for a pet, children learn to be tolerant, responsible and patient.
INTERVIEWER   What duties are involved? And what are the disadvantages of having a pet?
DR SPRINGER   Animals are living creatures and it's a big responsibility to look after them. Don't leave them alone for long periods of time. Think of buying two pets if you're not at home during the day. If you go on holiday, you'll have to ask someone to feed your pet and clean the litter-box.
INTERVIEWER   Can it affect my health to live with a pet?
DR SPRINGER   Many people have allergic reactions to animals. You should talk to a doctor before buying a pet. But pets also have a good effect on the health of their owners, for example when people take regular walks with their dogs.
INTERVIEWER   What costs will be involved?
DR SPRINGER   If you decide to have a companion in your home, quite a lot of money will go on food, vaccinations and other medical treatments, and insurance.
INTERVIEWER   I like exotic pets, such as snakes or lizards. What about them?
DR SPRINGER   Never buy pets that are imported from overseas, such as parrots, turtles or certain snakes. Most of these animals are caught and transported in terrible conditions and only a few survive the journey.
INTERVIEWER   Can there be problems with neighbours?
DR SPRINGER   If your cat likes exploring other gardens or if your dog keeps barking all day, you might have trouble with your neighbours. In some houses it is not allowed to have pets.
INTERVIEWER   Anything else I have to think of before buying a pet?
DR SPRINGER   All baby animals are sweet, but remember – they might grow to an enormous size, especially dogs.

Unit 12 Exercise 9

HANNAH Good morning, this is Hannah Cassidy. Can I speak to Ms Campbell please?
RECEPTIONIST Yes, one moment please.
MS CAMPBELL Ms Campbell speaking.
HANNAH Good morning, Ms Campbell, my name is Hannah Cassidy. I saw your ad in the paper this morning. I'm interested in the job as a shop assistant. Is it still vacant?
MS CAMPBELL Well, yes. There have been quite a few callers, but there hasn't been a final decision yet. Are you experienced in selling, Ms Cassidy?
HANNAH Yes, I've been selling fabrics in a shop in Princess Square for some years now but, unfortunately, they are closing down the shop at the end of the month.
MS CAMPBELL And how long have you been with that company?
HANNAH For over four and a half years. I started work there straight after I left school.
MS CAMPBELL Ah, I see. Now, a bit about us. We sell furniture as well as home textiles, china and tableware. Since you have experience in fabrics, home textiles could be the right department for you. Our shop is open Monday to Friday from 9.30 to 7, and on Saturday until 6. You would have one full day off every week but you would have to work every second Saturday. Could you manage that?
HANNAH Yes, of course. It's about the same with my present job. And – what about the pay? How much would that be?
MS CAMPBELL We can offer you £190 a week at the beginning. If you settle in well you can expect a rise after a couple of months. Would that be all right?
HANNAH Yes, that's fine. I'm really interested.
MS CAMPBELL Fine, Ms Cassidy. Could you come here for an interview with our personnel manager?
HANNAH Yes, of course. I've got Friday off this week, so I could come any time on Friday if that's all right.
MS CAMPBELL OK, could you be here at 2 pm?
HANNAH Yes, that'd be perfect.
MS CAMPBELL Do you know the address?
HANNAH It's in the High Gate shopping centre, isn't it?
MS CAMPBELL Yes, go to the first floor and ask for Mr Blackwell, he's the personnel manager… .

Business Correspondence, Exercise 5

MS POTTER Good morning, Scott. It's 6 am and I'm calling from the airport – I'm just about to catch my plane. Listen, my computer crashed last night while I was trying to write an e-mail and the mail can't wait until I get back so could you write it for me as soon as you get in. The address is on their letter – I've put it on your desk. OK, are you ready? "The subject is … er … Your order no. 582 of 2nd September.

Dear Ms Clarke, Thank you for your letter in which you informed us of an incorrect delivery. We are very sorry that we could not send you the correct quantity." Mmm, then we should give the reason for the delay. Let's see. "Unfortunately a strike in our factory caused a delay in production." OK, then tell her that she will receive all the goods she ordered within the next two weeks. Don't forget to apologize again for the delay. Oh and why don't you send her our new price list with our special offers for Christmas as an attachment? End it in the usual way, you know, Best regards etc. She's an important customer, so make sure you're polite – we don't want to lose her business. Thanks Scott and see you next week.

Unit word list

Diese neuen Wörter sind in der Reihenfolge ihres
Vorkommens im Text verzeichnet.
Es fehlen jedoch die Wörter, die zum Grundwortschatz
gehoren. (siehe *Basic Word List*)

Die Zahl am linken Rand gibt die Seitenzahl an.
p = das Wort befindet sich im *pairwork file*.
t = das Wort befindet sich im *transcript*.

Unit 1

6
in the sale	[ɪn ðə 'seɪl]	reduziert
up to	['ʌp tə]	bis zu
per cent	[pə'sent]	Prozent
sandal	['sændl]	Sandale
strap	[stræp]	Riemen
boring	['bɔːrɪŋ]	langweilig
beige	[beɪʒ]	beige
bargain	['bɑːgɪn]	günstiges Angebot
hurry up	[ˌhʌri 'ʌp]	sich beeilen

7
give sb a lift	[ˌgɪv ə 'lɪft]	jdn (mit dem Auto) mitnehmen
boot	[buːt]	Stiefel
suede	[sweɪd]	Wildleder
give back	[ˌgɪv 'bæk]	zurückgeben
prize	[praɪz]	Preis
coupon	['kuːpɒn]	Gutschein
satisfied	['sætɪsfaɪd]	zufrieden

8
describe	[dɪ'skraɪb]	beschreiben
ankle boot	['æŋkl buːt]	Halbstiefel
court shoe	['kɔːt ʃuː]	Pumps
hiking boot	['haɪkɪŋ buːt]	Wanderschuh
oxford (shoe)	['ɒksfəd]	geschnürter Halbschuh
platform soled shoe	['plætfɔːm səʊld ʃuː]	Schuh mit Plateausohle
slip-on shoe	['slɪpɒn ʃuː]	Slipper
sling back shoe	['slɪŋbæk ʃuː]	Slingbackschuh
strappy shoe	[ˌstræpi 'ʃuː]	Riemchenschuh
mule	[mjuːl]	Schlappen
lace-up shoe	['leɪs ʌp ʃuː]	Schnürschuh
knee-high	[ˌniː'haɪ]	kniehoch
upper	['ʌpə]	Oberteil
coated	['kəʊtɪd]	imprägniert
nubuck	['njuːbʌk]	Nubukleder
waxy	['wæksi]	(wachs)weich
patent leather	[ˌpætnt 'leðə]	Lackleder
synthetic	[sɪn'θetɪk]	synthetisch
canvas	['kænvəs]	Segeltuch
buckle	['bʌkl]	Schnalle
laces	['leɪsɪz]	Schnürsenkel
high-heeled	[ˌhaɪ'hiːld]	Stöckel-
medium heel	['miːdiəm hiːl]	halbhoher Absatz
low-heeled	[ˌləʊ 'hiːld]	mit niedrigen Absätzen
stiletto heel	[stɪ'letəʊ hiːl]	Pfennigabsatz
wedge heel	['wedʒ hiːl]	Keilabsatz
toe	[təʊ]	Spitze
waterproof	['wɔːtəpruːf]	wasserdicht
wide fitting	[ˌwaɪd 'fɪtɪŋ]	bequem passend
cleated sole	[ˌkliːtɪd 'səʊl]	Laufsohle
rubber	['rʌbə]	Gummi
hard-wearing	[ˌhɑːd'weərɪŋ]	strapazierfähig
padded	['pædɪd]	gefüttert
ankle collar	['æŋkl kɒlə]	Schaftrand
insole	['ɪnsəʊl]	Brand-, Einlegesohle
tongue	[tʌŋ]	Zunge
lining	['laɪnɪŋ]	Futter(stoff)
toe cap	['təʊ kæp]	Schuhkappe

9
turns, take sth in ~	[teɪk ɪn tɜːnz]	etw abwechselnd tun

9t
madam	['mædəm]	meine Dame
seat	[siːt]	(Sitz-)Platz
hurt	[hɜːt]	(sich) wehtun, schmerzen
straight away	[streɪt ə'weɪ]	sofort
plenty of	['plenti əv]	eine Menge, viel
ring up	[ˌrɪŋ 'ʌp]	anrufen

10
next to	['nekst tə]	(direkt) neben
middle	['mɪdl]	Mitte

11
half price, at ~	[ət hɑːf 'praɪs]	zum halben Preis
reduce	[rɪ'djuːs]	reduzieren
leatherware	['leðəweə]	Lederwaren
ski	[skiː]	Ski
binding	['baɪndɪŋ]	Bindung
item	['aɪtəm]	Artikel
impregnate	['ɪmpregneɪt]	imprägnieren
water-proofing	['wɔːtəpruːfɪŋ]	Imprägnier-
classic	['klæsɪk]	klassisch
occasion	[ə'keɪʒn]	Anlass, Gelegenheit

Unit 2

13
wellness	['welnəs]	Gesundheit, Wohlbefinden
test	[test]	prüfen, testen, (aus)probieren
apply to	[ə'plaɪ tə]	gelten/zutreffen für
exercise	['eksəsaɪz]	trainieren
at least	[ət 'liːst]	wenigstens, mindestens
than	[ðən]	als
none	[nʌn]	keine/r/s

at all [ət 'ɔːl]	überhaupt
overweight [ˌəʊvə'weɪt]	übergewichtig
underweight [ˌʌndə'weɪt]	untergewichtig
regularly ['regjələli]	regelmäßig
equivalent [ɪ'kwɪvələnt]	Entsprechung
processed food [ˌprəʊsest 'fuːd]	industriell hergestellte Nahrungsmittel
white bread [waɪt 'bred]	Weißbrot
day off [ˌdeɪ 'ɒf]	freier Tag
at home [ət 'həʊm]	zu Hause
TV, watch~ [wɒtʃ ˌtiːˈviː]	fernsehen
lie [laɪ]	liegen
outdoor ['aʊtdɔː]	im Freien
activity [æk'tɪvəti]	Aktivität, Tätigkeit
in-line skating ['ɪnlaɪn skeɪtɪŋ]	Inlineskaten

14

scores [skɔːz]	Punkt(estand)
care about ['keər əbaʊt]	sich kümmern um
need [niːd]	Bedürfnis
look after [lʊk 'ɑːftə]	aufpassen auf
serious ['sɪəriəs]	schwer, ernsthaft
regular ['regjələ]	regelmäßig
exercise ['eksəsaɪz]	körperliche Bewegung
depression [dɪ'preʃn]	Depression
anxiety [æŋ'zaɪəti]	Angst(zustand)
lead to ['liːd tə]	führen zu
productivity [ˌprɒdʌk'tɪvəti]	Produktivität
at work [ət 'wɜːk]	bei der Arbeit
increase [ɪn'kriːs]	steigern
gradually ['grædʒuəli]	allmählich, nach und nach
diet ['daɪət]	Ernährung
junk food ['dʒʌŋk fuːd]	minderwertiges Essen
in advance [ɪn əd'vɑːns]	im Voraus
cope with ['kəʊp wɪð]	fertig werden mit
relax [rɪ'læks]	(sich) entspannen
tense [tens]	angespannt, nervös
even ['iːvn]	sogar (noch)
make friends [meɪk 'frendz]	Freunde finden
congratulations [kənˌgrætʃu'leɪʃnz]	herzlichen Glückwunsch
shape [ʃeɪp]	Form, Verfassung
advantage [əd'vɑːntɪdʒ]	Vorzug
balanced ['bælənst]	ausgewogen
overdo [ˌəʊvə'duː]	übertreiben
develop [dɪ'veləp]	entwickeln
social ['səʊʃl]	sozial, gesellschaftlich
intellectual [ˌɪntə'lektʃʊəl]	intellektuell

15

unscramble [ˌʌn'skræmbl]	in die richtige Reihenfolge bringen
fluid ['fluːɪd]	Flüssigkeit

16

body, part of the ~ [pɑːt əv ðə'bɒdi]	Körperteil
drawing ['drɔːɪŋ]	Zeichnung
back ['bæk]	Rücken
bottom ['bɒtəm]	Hintern
calf [kɑːf]	Wade
chest [tʃest]	Brust
ear [ɪə]	Ohr
elbow ['elbəʊ]	Ellbogen
finger ['fɪŋgə]	Finger
head [hed]	Kopf
hips [hɪps]	Hüften
knee [niː]	Knie
leg [leg]	Bein
spine [spaɪn]	Rückgrat
stomach ['stʌmək]	Magen
toe [təʊ]	Zehe
thigh [θaɪ]	(Ober-)Schenkel
wrist [rɪst]	Handgelenk
drawing ['drɔːɪŋ]	Zeichnung
clearly ['klɪəli]	klar
brain [breɪn]	Gehirn
mental ['mentl]	geistig
palm [pɑːm]	Handfläche
spinal ['spaɪnl]	Rückgrat-
boost [buːst]	erhöhen, verstärken
blood [blʌd]	Blut
flow [fləʊ]	Zufluss, Fluss
move [muːv]	Bewegung
stand [stænd]	stehen, sich hinstellen
erect [ɪ'rekt]	aufrecht
outstretched [ˌaʊt'stretʃt]	ausgestreckt
in line with [ɪn 'laɪn wɪð]	in einer Linie mit
picture ['pɪktʃə]	sich vorstellen
spin [spɪn]	(sich schnell) drehen
clockwise ['klɒkwaɪz]	im Uhrzeigersinn
direction [də'rekʃn]	Richtung
build up [ˌbɪld 'ʌp]	steigern
speed [spiːd]	Geschwindigkeit
slow down [sləʊ daʊn]	langsamer werden
focus ['fəʊkəs]	konzentrieren
vision ['vɪʒn]	Blick
single ['sɪŋgl]	einzeln
point [pɔɪnt]	Punkt
ahead of [ə'hed əv]	vor
prevent [prɪ'vent]	(ver)hindern, verhüten
dizzy ['dɪzi]	schwindlig
enhance [ɪn'hɑːns]	erhöhen, steigern
circulation [ˌsɜːkjə'leɪʃn]	Kreislauf
energy ['enədʒi]	Energie
aid [eɪd]	helfen
spinal fluid [ˌspaɪnl 'fluːɪd]	Rückenmarksflüssigkeit
contribute [kən'trɪbjuːt]	beitragen
clarity ['klærəti]	Klarheit

17

serious, be ~ about [bi 'sɪəriəs əbaʊt]	etw im Ernst tun wollen
terrible ['terəbl]	schrecklich, furchtbar
ill [ɪl]	krank
news [njuːz]	Neuigkeit(en)
organize ['ɔːgənaɪz]	organisieren

18

DJ [ˌdiː 'dʒeɪ]	Diskjockey
listener ['lɪsnə]	Zuhörer/in
physical ['fɪzɪkl]	körperlich
inactive [ɪn'æktɪv]	inaktiv
risk [rɪsk]	Risiko
heart disease ['hɑːt dɪziːz]	Herzkrankheit
inactivity [ˌɪnæk'tɪvəti]	Inaktivität
factor ['fæktə]	Faktor
diabetes [ˌdaɪə'biːtiːz]	Zuckerkrankheit
cholesterol [kə'lestərɒl]	Cholesterin
extremely [ɪk'striːmli]	sehr, äußerst
strengthen ['streŋθn]	stärken
lungs [lʌŋz]	Lungen
make sb do sth [meɪk 'duː]	jdn dazu veranlassen/bringen, etw zu tun

burn	[bɜːn]	verbrennen	
calorie	['kæləri]	Kalorie	
build	[bɪld]	(auf)bauen	
bone	[bəʊn]	Knochen	
joint	[dʒɔɪnt]	Gelenk	
muscle	['mʌsl]	Muskel	
blood pressure	['blʌd preʃə]	Blutdruck	
lower	['ləʊə]	senken	
level	['levl]	Spiegel	
involved in	[ɪn'vɒlvd ɪn]	bezüglich	
pleasant	['pleznt]	angenehm	
experience	[ɪk'spɪəriəns]	Erlebnis	
consult	[kən'sʌlt]	konsultieren, sich wenden an	
doctor	['dɒktə]	Arzt, Ärztin	
pain	[peɪn]	Schmerz	
breathless	['breθləs]	außer Atem	
pick	[pɪk]	auswählen	
sb is likely to do sth	[ɪz 'laɪkli tə duː]	jd wird etw wahrscheinlich tun	
stay with	['steɪ wɪð]	bleiben bei	
brisk	[brɪsk]	lebhaft, kräftig	
aerobics	[eə'rəʊbɪks]	Aerobik	
dancing	['dɑːnsɪŋ]	Tanzen	
cross-country skiing	[ˌkrɒs 'kʌntri skiːɪŋ]	Skilanglauf	
skating	['skeɪtɪŋ]	Eislauf	
jogging	['dʒɒgɪŋ]	Jogging, Dauerlauf	
swimming	['swɪmɪŋ]	Schwimmen	
equip	[ɪ'kwɪp]	ausrüsten, ausstatten	
require	[rɪ'kwaɪə]	benötigen, erfordern	
equipment	[ɪ'kwɪpmənt]	Ausrüstung	
appropriate	[ə'prəʊpriət]	geeignet, angemessen, passend	
weather	['weðə]	Wetter	
rubberized	['rʌbəraɪzd]	gummiert	
nonporous	[ˌnɒn'pɔːrəs]	nicht porös	
last	[lɑːst]	letzte(r,s)	
piece of advice	[piːs əv əd'vaɪs]	ein Ratschlag	
caller	['kɔːlə]	Anrufer/in	

19

hooded	['hʊdɪd]	mit Kapuze	
sweat	[swet]	Schweiß	
front	[frʌnt]	Vorder-	
pocket	['pɒkɪt]	Tasche	
sleeve	[sliːv]	Ärmel	
drawcord	['drɔːkɔːd]	Kordelzugband	
washable	['wɒʃəbl]	waschbar	
tracksuit	['træksuːt]	Jogginganzug	
elasticated	[ɪ'læstɪkeɪtɪd]	elastisch	
tape	[teɪp]	Band	
detail	['diːteɪl]	Einzelheit, Detail	
jersey	['dʒɜːzi]	Jersey	
lycra	['laɪkrə]	Lycra	
perfect	['pɜːfɪkt]	vollkommen, perfekt	
fit	[fɪt]	passen (zu); Passform	
tank top	['tæŋk tɒp]	Pullunder	
fleece top	['fliːs tɒp]	Fleeceshirt	
embroidered	[ɪm'brɔɪdəd]	bestickt	
polar fleece	[ˌpəʊlə 'fliːs]	Thermofleece	
lilac	['laɪlək]	lila	
cherry	['tʃeri]	kirschrot	
zip fastening	['zɪp fɑːsnɪŋ]	mit Reißverschluss	
bottoms	['bɒtəmz]	Hose	

20

sports	[spɔːts]	Sport-	
whole	[həʊl]	ganze/r/s	
cash desk	['kæʃ desk]	Kasse	
sportswear	['spɔːtsweə]	Sportkleidung	
care instructions	[ˌkeər ɪn'strʌkʃnz]	Pflegeanleitung	
advertise	['ædvətaɪz]	werben (für)	

Unit 3

21

spare time	[ˌspeə 'taɪm]	Freizeit	
paint	[peɪnt]	malen	
play	[pleɪ]	spielen	
sew	[səʊ]	nähen	
photos, take ~	['teɪk fəʊtəʊz]	fotografieren	
windsurfing	['wɪndsɜːfɪŋ]	Surfen	
team	[tiːm]	Mannschaft	
play on a team	[pleɪ ɒn ə 'tiːm]	in einer Mannschaft spielen	
design	[dɪ'zaɪn]	entwerfen	

21t

succeed in	[sək'siːd ɪn]	gelingen	
create	[kri'eɪt]	(er)schaffen	
attend	[ə'tend]	teilnehmen an, besuchen	
evening course	['iːvnɪŋ kɔːs]	Abendkurs	
fashion design	['fæʃn dɪzaɪn]	Modedesign	
evening class	['iːvnɪŋ klɑːs]	Abendschulkurs	
language	['læŋgwɪdʒ]	Sprache	
a little	[ə 'lɪtl]	ein wenig, ein bisschen	
notice	['nəʊtɪs]	(be)merken	
good, be~ at sth	[bi 'gʊd ət]	gut in etw sein	
study	['stʌdi]	lernen, studieren	
climbing	['klaɪmɪŋ]	Bergsteigen	
keen on	['kiːn ɒn]	wild auf	
refuse	[rɪ'fjuːz]	ablehnen, sich weigern	
explore	[ɪk'splɔː]	erforschen, erkunden	
countryside	['kʌntrisaɪd]	Landschaft	
thrilling	['θrɪlɪŋ]	aufregend	
feeling	['fiːlɪŋ]	Gefühl	
adventure	[əd'ventʃə]	Abenteuer	
spend	[spend]	verbringen	
Alps, the ~	[ðɪ 'ælps]	die Alpen	
reduction	[rɪ'dʌkʃn]	Ermäßigung	
afford	[ə'fɔːd]	sich leisten (können)	
indoors	['ɪndɔːz]	innen	
local	['ləʊkl]	örtlich	
match	[mætʃ]	Spiel	
miss out on	[ˌmɪs 'aʊt ɒn]	verpassen	
league	[liːg]	Liga	
win	[wɪn]	gewinnen	

22

fail	[feɪl]	scheitern	
semi-final	[ˌsemi'faɪnl]	Halbfinale	
practise	['præktɪs]	(ein)üben	
textile	['tekstaɪl]	Textilie	
opera	['ɒprə]	Oper	
classical	['klæsɪkl]	klassisch	
race	[reɪs]	(Wett-)Rennen	

23

step	[step]	Schritt	

English	IPA	German
right	[raɪt]	genau
technique	[tek'ni:k]	Technik
one-to-one lesson	[ˌwʌn tə 'wʌn 'lesn]	Einzel-(Unterrichts-)Stunde
professional	[prə'feʃənl]	Profi
difference	['dɪfrəns]	Unterschied
mid-sized	[ˌmɪd'saɪzd]	mittlerer Größe
lightweight	['laɪtweɪt]	Leicht-
graphite	['græfaɪt]	Graphit
according to	[ə'kɔ:dɪŋ tə]	entsprechend
indoor court	['ɪndɔ: kɔ:t]	Hallenplatz
tread	[tred]	Profil
outdoor court	[ˌaʊtdɔ: 'kɔ:t]	Platz im Freien
club	[klʌb]	Klub, Verein
tennis whites	[ˌtenɪs 'waɪts]	weiße Tenniskleidung
begin, to ~ with	[tə bɪ'gɪn wɪð]	zunächst, anfangs
chance	[tʃɑ:ns]	Chance, Gelegenheit
hit	[hɪt]	schlagen, treffen
area	['eərɪə]	Bereich
ultimate	['ʌltɪmət]	allerletzte/r/s, allergrößte/r/s
challenge	['tʃælɪndʒ]	Herausforderung
join	[dʒɔɪn]	beitreten
tournament	['tʊənəmənt]	Turnier

24

English	IPA	German
bicycle, bike	['baɪsɪkl, baɪk]	Fahrrad
vary	['veəri]	sich unterscheiden, variieren
strong	[strɒŋ]	kräftig (gebaut)
at the same time	[ət ðə seɪm 'taɪm]	gleichzeitig
gear	[gɪə]	Gang
awful	['ɔ:fl]	furchtbar, schrecklich
passionate	['pæʃənət]	leidenschaftlich
biker	['baɪkə]	Radfahrer/in
worth	[wɜ:θ]	wert
ride	[raɪd]	fahren (mit)
trip	[trɪp]	Ausflug, Fahrt
surrounding	[sə'raʊndɪŋ]	umgebend, umliegend
around here	[əˌraʊnd 'hɪə]	hier herum
although	[ɔ:l'ðəʊ]	obwohl
pity, what a ~	[wɒt ə 'pɪti]	wie schade
theft	[θeft]	Diebstahl
lock	[lɒk]	abschließen
combination lock	[ˌkɒmbɪ'neɪʃn lɒk]	Kombinationsschloss
secure	[sɪ'kjʊə]	sicher
shackle lock	['ʃækl lɒk]	Bügelschloss
combine	[kəm'baɪn]	verbinden
styling	['staɪlɪŋ]	Gestaltung
technology	[tek'nɒlədʒi]	Technik, Technologie
inch	[ɪntʃ]	Zoll
mudguard	['mʌdgɑ:d]	Schutzblech
prop stand	['prɒp stænd]	Fahrradständer
attach	[ə'tætʃ]	anbringen
luggage carrier	['lʌgɪdʒ kærɪə]	Gepäckträger

25

English	IPA	German
car park	['kɑ: pɑ:k]	Parkplatz
driving licence	['draɪvɪŋlaɪsns]	Führerschein
try out	[ˌtraɪ 'aʊt]	(aus)probieren
bell	[bel]	Klingel
chain cover	['tʃeɪn kʌvə]	Kettenschutz
fork	[fɔ:k]	Gabel
frame	[freɪm]	Rahmen
brake	[breɪk]	Bremse
gear levers	['gɪə li:vəz]	Gangschaltung
handlebars	['hændlbɑ:z]	Lenker
headlamp	['hedlæmp]	Scheinwerfer, Lampe
pedal	['pedl]	Pedal
pump	[pʌmp]	Pumpe
rear	[rɪə]	Hinter(rad)-
reflector	[rɪ'flektə]	Rückstrahler
rim	[rɪm]	Felge
saddle	['sædl]	Sattel
tyre	['taɪə]	Reifen

26

English	IPA	German
wonderful	['wʌndəfl]	wunderbar, -voll
at the seaside	[ət ðə 'si:saɪd]	am Meer
divorced	[dɪ'vɔ:st]	geschieden
neighbour	['neɪbə]	Nachbar/in
unemployed	[ˌʌnɪm'plɔɪd]	arbeitslos

27

English	IPA	German
inform	[ɪn'fɔ:m]	informieren, benachrichtigen
teacher	['ti:tʃə]	Lehrer/in
reminder	[rɪ'maɪndə]	Mahnung
company	['kʌmpəni]	Firma

Unit 4

28

English	IPA	German
own, of one's ~	[əv wʌnz 'əʊn]	eigen
share	[ʃeə]	(sich) teilen, gemeinsam nutzen
lane	[leɪn]	Gasse, Weg
bathroom	['bɑ:θru:m]	Badezimmer
per week	[pə 'wi:k]	pro Woche
heating	['hi:tɪŋ]	Heizung
central heating	[ˌsentrəl 'hi:tɪŋ]	Zentralheizung
lounge	[laʊndʒ]	Wohnzimmer, Salon
deposit	[dɪ'pɒzɪt]	Anzahlung, Kaution

28t

English	IPA	German
nobody	['nəʊbədi]	niemand
not yet	[nɒt 'jet]	noch nicht
semi-detached house	[ˌsemi dɪ'tætʃt haʊs]	Doppelhaushälfte
gas central heating	[gæs ˌsentrəl 'hi:tɪŋ]	Gaszentralheizung
secretary	['sekrətri]	Sekretär/in
by the way	[baɪ ðə 'weɪ]	übrigens, nebenbei
working hours	[ˌwɜ:kɪŋ 'aʊəz]	Arbeitszeit

28

English	IPA	German
bedroom	['bedru:m]	Schlafzimmer
detached house	[dɪ'tætʃt haʊs]	freistehendes Haus
balcony	['bælkəni]	Balkon

29

English	IPA	German
bay window	[ˌbeɪ 'wɪndəʊ]	Erkerfenster
chimney	['tʃɪmni]	Schornstein
doorbell	['dɔ:bel]	Türklingel
fence	[fens]	Zaun
front door	[ˌfrʌnt 'dɔ:]	Haustür
hall	[hɔ:l]	Flur, Diele

aerial	['eəriəl]	Antenne
window sill	['wɪndəʊsɪl]	Fensterbrett

30

landlady	['lændleɪdi]	Wirtin, Vermieterin
grass	[grɑːs]	Gras, Rasen
put up	[ˌpʊt 'ʌp]	anbringen
wallpaper	['wɔːlpeɪpə]	Tapete
painting	['peɪntɪŋ]	Malerarbeiten
unfurnished	[ʌn'fɜːnɪʃt]	unmöbliert
wardrobe	['wɔːdrəʊb]	Kleiderschrank
bookshelf	['bʊkʃelf]	(Bücher-)Regal
keep	[kiːp]	behalten
turn into	[ˌtɜːn 'ɪntə]	(sich) verwandeln in
complicated	['kɒmplɪkeɪtɪd]	kompliziert
ugly	['ʌgli]	hässlich
curtain	['kɜːtn]	Vorhang, Gardine

31

alter	['ɔːltə]	ändern
dye	[daɪ]	färben
lay	[leɪ]	(ver)legen
tap	[tæp]	Wasserhahn
drip	[drɪp]	tropfen

32

pick out	[ˌpɪk 'aʊt]	aussuchen
sofa bed	['səʊfə bed]	Sofabett
living room	['lɪvɪŋ ruːm]	Wohnzimmer
cream	[kriːm]	creme(farbig)
stripe	[straɪp]	Streifen
shade	[ʃeɪd]	(Farb-)Ton
clash	[klæʃ]	nicht harmonieren, sich beißen
cover	['kʌvə]	Überzug
remove	[rɪ'muːv]	entfernen, abziehen
non-iron	[ˌnɒn 'aɪən]	bügelfrei
nasty	['nɑːsti]	hässlich
stain	[steɪn]	Fleck

33

treatment	['triːtmənt]	Behandlung
nappa leather	['næpə leðə]	Nappaleder
durable	['djʊərəbl]	dauerhaft, haltbar
be worried about	[bi 'wʌrɪd əbaʊt]	besorgt sein um
laugh	[lɑːf]	lachen
haircut	['heəkʌt]	Haarschnitt
cry	[kraɪ]	weinen
give up	[ˌgɪv 'ʌp]	aufgeben
exhausted	[ɪg'zɔːstɪd]	erschöpft
sad	[sæd]	traurig
gym teacher	['dʒɪm tiːtʃə]	Sportlehrer/in
mirror	['mɪrə]	Spiegel
chest of drawers	[ˌtʃest əv 'drɔːz]	Kommode

34

extract	['ekstrækt]	Auszug
ready-made	[ˌredi 'meɪd]	Fertig-
satin	['sætɪn]	Satin
latest	['leɪtɪst]	neueste(r,s)
tab-top	['tæbtɒp]	Schlaufe
heading tape	['hedɪŋ teɪp]	Vorhangband
valance	['væləns]	Volant
tie-back	['taɪbæk]	Raffhalter
ocean	['əʊʃn]	Meer
rail	[reɪl]	Schiene

width	[wɪdθ]	Breite

35

comfort	['kʌmfət]	Bequemlichkeit
quality	['kwɒləti]	Qualität
construction	[kən'strʌkʃn]	Bau, Konstruktion
priority	[praɪ'ɒrəti]	Vorrang, Priorität
consider	[kən'sɪdə]	erwägen
upholstered	[ʌp'həʊlstəd]	gepolstert
padding	['pædɪŋ]	Polsterung
deck	[dek]	Federung
specification	[ˌspesɪfɪ'keɪʃn]	Vor-, Angabe
punishment	['pʌnɪʃmənt]	starke Beanspruchung
opt	[ɒpt]	sich entscheiden
weave	[wiːv]	weben
rayon	['reɪɒn]	Kunstseide
chenille	[ʃə'niːl]	Chenille
blend	[blend]	Mischung, Gemisch
treat	[triːt]	behandeln
mill	[mɪl]	Spinnerei
stain-repellent	[ˌsteɪn rɪ'pelənt]	schmutzabweisend
cushion	['kʊʃn]	Kissen
density	['densəti]	Dichte
foam rubber	[ˌfəʊm 'rʌbə]	Schaumgummi
provide	[prə'vaɪd]	bieten, sorgen für
support	[sə'pɔːt]	Halt
weigh	[weɪ]	wiegen
square inch	[ˌskweər 'ɪntʃ]	Quadratzoll
tag	['tæg]	Etikett
maximum	['mæksɪməm]	höchste/r/s
protect from	[prə'tekt frəm]	schützen vor
fray	[freɪ]	abnutzen, ausfransen
kiln-dried	['kɪln draɪd]	im Ofen getrocknet
hardwood	['hɑːdwʊd]	Hartholz
oak	[əʊk]	Eiche
maple	['meɪpl]	Ahorn
ash	[æʃ]	Esche
dowel	['daʊəl]	Dübel
corner block	['kɔːnə blɒk]	Eckversteifung
screw	[skruː]	schrauben
strength	[streŋθ]	Stärke
hand-tied	[ˌhænd'taɪd]	handbefestigt
coil	[kɔɪl]	Spirale
cone spring	['kəʊn sprɪŋ]	Sprungfeder
adequate	['ædɪkwət]	ausreichend
extra	['ekstrə]	zusätzlich
resilience	[rɪ'zɪliəns]	Elastizität

36

move into	[muːv 'ɪntə]	einziehen
pony tail	['pəʊni teɪl]	Pferdeschwanz
slim	[slɪm]	schlank
moustache	[mə'stɑːʃ]	Schnurrbart
expert	['ekspɜːt]	Experte/Expertin
plaster	['plɑːstə]	Gips
accident	['æksɪdənt]	Unfall

Unit 5

37t

hyphen	['haɪfn]	Bindestrich
as soon as	[əz 'suːn əz]	sobald

37

dictate	[dɪk'teɪt]	diktieren

38

by phone	[baɪ 'fəʊn]	telefonisch

order, place an ~ [ˌpleɪs ənˈɔːdə]	eine Bestellung aufgeben, bestellen	variable [ˈveərɪəbl]	verstellbar
tableware [ˈteɪblweə]	Tafelgeschirr	slicing [ˈslaɪsɪŋ]	Schnittstärke
order form [ˈɔːdə fɔːm]	Bestellformular	control [kənˈtrəʊl]	Regler
description [dɪˈskrɪpʃn]	Beschreibung	press and hold switch [ˌpres ənd ˈhəʊld swɪtʃ]	Sicherheitsschalter
reference number [ˈrefərəns nʌmbə]	Bestellnummer	folding [ˈfəʊldɪŋ]	zusammenklappbar
quantity [ˈkwɒntəti]	Menge	protect [prəˈtekt]	schützen
total [ˈtəʊtl]	Gesamt(preis)	compact [ˈkɒmpækt]	kompakt
subtotal [ˈsʌbtəʊtl]	Zwischensumme	facility [fəˈsɪləti]	Vorrichtung
charge [tʃɑːdʒ]	Kosten, Gebühr	thick [θɪk]	dick
expiry date [ɪkˈspaɪəri deɪt]	Verfallsdatum	thin [θɪn]	dünn
cheque [tʃek]	Scheck	electronic [ˌɪlekˈtrɒnɪk]	elektronisch
dinner plate [ˈdɪnə pleɪt]	großer Teller	browning control [ˌbraʊnɪŋ kənˈtrəʊl]	Bräunungsregler
dessert plate [dɪˈzɜːt pleɪt]	Dessertteller	high-lift facility [ˌhaɪlɪft fəˈsɪləti]	Hebevorrichtung
diameter [daɪˈæmɪtə]	Durchmesser	toasting chamber [ˈtəʊstɪŋ tʃeɪmbə]	Toastkammer
mug [mʌg]	Becher(tasse)	crumb tray [ˈkrʌm treɪ]	Krümelschale
height [haɪt]	Höhe, Größe	detachable [dɪˈtætʃəbl]	abnehmbar
salt mill [ˈsɔːlt mɪl]	Salzmühle	blender [ˈblendə]	Mischer, Mixer
pepper mill [ˈpepə mɪl]	Pfeffermühle	attachment [əˈtætʃmənt]	Aufsatz
gravy boat [ˈgreɪvi bəʊt]	Sauciere	pulse action [ˈpʌls ækʃn]	pulsierende/stampfende Arbeitsweise
stand [stænd]	Tablett	dishwasher safe [ˈdɪʃwɒʃə seɪf]	spülmaschinenfest
salad bowl [ˈsæləd bəʊl]	Salatschüssel	chopping blade [ˈtʃɒpɪŋ bleɪd]	Schneidemesser
napkin [ˈnæpkɪn]	Serviette	disc [dɪsk]	Platte, Scheibe
pack of four [pæk əv ˈfɔː]	Viererpack	shred [ʃred]	zerkleinern
oval [ˈəʊvl]	oval	slice [slaɪs]	schneiden
platter [ˈplætə]	Platte	chip [tʃɪp]	schnitzeln
teapot [ˈtiːpɒt]	Teekanne	pint [paɪnt]	Pint
capacity [kəˈpæsəti]	Fassungsvermögen	sharp [ʃɑːp]	scharf
saucer [ˈsɔːsə]	Untertasse	tough [tʌf]	robust

38t

connect [kəˈnekt]	verbinden	almost [ˈɔːlməʊst]	fast, beinahe
crockery [ˈkrɒkəri]	Geschirr	rapid [ˈræpɪd]	Schnell-
just in case [dʒʌst ɪn ˈkeɪs]	nur für den Fall	conceal [kənˈsiːl]	verbergen
contact [ˈkɒntækt]	sich in Verbindung setzen mit	element [ˈelɪmənt]	Element
		limescale [ˈlaɪmskeɪl]	Kalkstein
charge [tʃɑːdʒ]	berechnen	indicator [ˈɪndɪkeɪtə]	Anzeige
in stock [ɪn ˈstɒk]	vorrätig	non-slip [ˌnɒn ˈslɪp]	rutschfest

40

household gadget [ˌhaʊshəʊld ˈgædʒɪt]	Haushaltsgerät	comprise [kəmˈpraɪz]	umfassen, bestehen aus
coffee-maker [ˈkɒfimeɪkə]	Kaffeemaschine	ladle [ˈleɪdl]	Schöpfkelle
food slicer [ˈfuːd slaɪsə]	Allesschneider	turner [ˈtɜːnə]	Wender
kettle [ˈketl]	Wasserkocher	sieve [sɪv]	Sieb
multi-purpose knife [ˌmʌltiˈpɜːpəs naɪf]	Kombimesser	whisk [wɪsk]	Schneebesen
pan set [ˈpæn set]	Kochtopfset	grater [ˈgreɪtə]	Reibe
food processor [ˈfuːd prəʊsesə]	Küchenmaschine	triple [ˈtrɪpl]	dreifach
tool [tuːl]	Werkzeug	overpressure [ˌəʊvəˈpreʃə]	Überdruck
gauge [geɪdʒ]	Anzeige	device [dɪˈvaɪs]	Vorrichtung
permanent [ˈpɜːmənənt]	permanent	opening [ˈəʊpnɪŋ]	Öffnen
stainless steel [ˌsteɪnləs ˈstiːl]	rostfreier Stahl	release [rɪˈliːs]	freisetzen
safety pressure valve [ˌseɪfti ˈpreʃə vælv]	Überdruckventil	electric [ɪˈlektrɪk]	elektrisch
		hob [hɒb]	Herdplatte
cord storage [kɔːd ˈstɔːrɪdʒ]	Kabelfach	guarantee [ˌgærənˈtiː]	Garantie
base [beɪs]	Fuß	cookbook [ˈkʊkbʊk]	Kochbuch
lid [lɪd]	Deckel	saucepan [ˈsɔːspən]	Kochtopf
removable [rɪˈmuːvəbl]	abnehmbar	milk pan [ˈmɪlk pæn]	Milchtopf
blade [bleɪd]	Klinge	frying pan [ˈfraɪɪŋ pæn]	Bratpfanne
slide [slaɪd]	gleiten		
carriage [ˈkærɪdʒ]	Schlitten		
protection [prəˈtekʃn]	Schutz		
grip [grɪp]	Griff		

41

able, to be ~ to [bi ˈeɪbl tə]	können
unplug [ˌʌnˈplʌg]	den Stecker herausziehen

42

present [ˈpreznt]	Geschenk

own, on one's [ɒn wʌnz 'əʊn]	allein
plug in [ˌplʌg 'ɪn]	anschließen
dangerous ['deɪndʒərəs]	gefährlich
wet [wet]	nass, feucht
included [ɪn'kluːdɪd]	eingeschlossen, enthalten
damage ['dæmɪdʒ]	beschädigen
non-stick [ˌnɒn'stɪk]	teflonbeschichtet
distribute [dɪ'strɪbjuːt]	verteilen

43

prepare [prɪ'peə]	vorbereiten
refrigerate [rɪ'frɪdʒəreɪt]	kühlen
stir [stɜː]	(um)rühren
whip [wɪp]	schlagen
trifle ['traɪfl]	Biskuit-Nachspeise
sponge cake ['spʌndʒ keɪk]	Biskuitkuchen
jelly ['dʒeli]	Wackelpeter
powder ['paʊdə]	Pulver
vanilla [və'nɪlə]	Vanille
flavour ['fleɪvə]	Geschmack
peach [piːtʃ]	Pfirsich
drain [dreɪn]	ablaufen lassen
icing sugar ['aɪsɪŋ ʃʊgə]	Puderzucker
serving dish ['sɜːvɪŋ dɪʃ]	Servierschüssel
drizzle ['drɪzl]	träufeln
crystal ['krɪstl]	Kristall
dissolve [dɪ'zɒlv]	(sich) auflösen
heat [hiːt]	Hitze, Wärme
surface ['sɜːfɪs]	Oberfläche
cool [kuːl]	(ab)kühlen
decoratively ['dekərətɪvli]	dekorativ

Unit 6

44

household chores [ˌhaʊshəʊld 'tʃɔːz]	Hausarbeiten
drill [drɪl]	bohren
hole [həʊl]	Loch
wall [wɔːl]	Wand, Mauer
dust [dʌst]	Staub wischen
bulb [bʌlb]	Glühbirne
sew on [ˌsəʊ 'ɒn]	annähen
vacuum-cleaning ['vækjuəm kliːnɪŋ]	Staubsaugen
washing-up [ˌwɒʃɪŋ'ʌp]	Abwasch
role [rəʊl]	Rolle
nowadays ['naʊədeɪz]	heutzutage
full-time [ˌfʊl 'taɪm]	Vollzeit-, Ganztags-
unable [ʌn'eɪbl]	unfähig, nicht in der Lage
necessary ['nesəsəri]	nötig, notwendig
helpless ['helpləs]	hilflos
alone [ə'ləʊn]	allein(e)
turn on [ˌtɜːn 'ɒn]	einschalten
vice versa [ˌvaɪs 'vɜːsə]	umgekehrt
be aware [bi ə'weə]	sich bewusst sein
reverse [rɪ'vɜːs]	umkehren
expectation [ˌekspek'teɪʃn]	Erwartung
iron ['aɪən]	bügeln
flexible ['fleksəbl]	flexibel
housework ['haʊswɜːk]	Hausarbeit(en)
compromise ['kɒmprəmaɪz]	Kompromiss
unloved [ˌʌn'lʌvd]	ungeliebt
basis ['beɪsɪs]	Basis
relationship [rɪ'leɪʃnʃɪp]	Beziehung

45

progress ['prəʊgres]	Fortschritt/e
imagine [ɪ'mædʒɪn]	sich vorstellen
especially [ɪ'speʃəli]	besonders
kitchen sink ['kɪtʃɪn sɪŋk]	Küchenspüle
top-class performance [ˌtɒpklɑːs pə'fɔːməns]	hervorragende Leistung(en)
minimum ['mɪnɪməm]	minimal
kWh [ˌkeɪ dʌbljuː 'eɪtʃ]	Kilowattstunde
consumption [kən'sʌmpʃn]	Verbrauch
economy [ɪ'kɒnəmi]	Sparprogramm
delicate ['delɪkət]	empfindlich
load [ləʊd]	Ladung, Füllung
high performance [ˌhaɪ pə'fɔːməns]	Hochleistungs-
jet [dʒet]	Düse
dried-on [ˌdraɪd 'ɒn]	angetrocknet
operation [ˌɒpə'reɪʃn]	Betrieb
decibel ['desɪbel]	Dezibel
interior [ɪn'tɪəriə]	Innere(s), Innenausstattung
place setting ['pleɪs setɪŋ]	Gedeck
operate ['ɒpəreɪt]	bedienen
additional [ə'dɪʃənl]	zusätzlich
child-safety catch [tʃaɪld 'seɪfti kætʃ]	Kindersicherung
anti-flood system [ˌænti 'flʌd sɪstəm]	Überlaufschutz
rust-free [ˌrʌst'friː]	rostfrei
extend [ɪk'stend]	verlängern

46

vacuum ['vækjuəm]	(staub)saugen
by hand [baɪ 'hænd]	mit der Hand
hang up [ˌhæŋ 'ʌp]	aufhängen
line [laɪn]	(Wäsche-)Leine
on test [ɒn 'test]	im Test
rely on [rɪ'laɪ ɒn]	sich verlassen auf

47

at a glance [ət ə 'glɑːns]	auf einen Blick
guide [gaɪd]	Führer/in
reliable [rɪ'laɪəbl]	zuverlässig
major ['meɪdʒə]	bedeutend
wise [waɪz]	weise, klug
highlight ['haɪlaɪt]	hervorheben
point out [ˌpɔɪnt 'aʊt]	hinweisen auf
suffer ['sʌfə]	leiden
be based on [bi 'beɪst ɒn]	basieren auf
break down [ˌbreɪk 'daʊn]	versagen
previous ['priːviəs]	vergangen
likely ['laɪkli]	wahrscheinlich
rank [ræŋk]	einstufen
average ['ævərɪdʒ]	durchschnittlich
fault [fɔːlt]	Defekt
VCR [ˌviː siː 'ɑː]	Videorekorder
survey ['sɜːveɪ]	Umfrage
leak [liːk]	undichte Stelle
account for [ə'kaʊnt fə]	ausmachen
dual-function [ˌdjuːəl 'fʌŋkʃn]	Doppelfunktion
wash-dryer ['wɒʃdraɪə]	Waschmaschine mit Trockenschleuder
unusual [ʌn'juːʒʊəl]	ungewöhnlich
noise [nɔɪz]	Geräusch
cylinder cleaner ['sɪlɪndə kliːnə]	Bodenstaubsauger
upright ['ʌpraɪt]	aufrecht

microwave oven	[ˌmaɪkrəweɪv 'ʌvn]	Mikrowelle
chest	[tʃest]	Truhe

49
switch off	[ˌswɪtʃ 'ɒf]	ausschalten
turn down	[ˌtɜːn 'daʊn]	leiser stellen
switch on	[ˌswɪtʃ 'ɒn]	einschalten
operating instructions	[ˌɒpəreɪtɪŋ ɪn'strʌkʃnz]	Bedienungsanleitung
function	['fʌŋkʃn]	Funktion
remote control handset	[rɪˌməʊt kən'trəʊl hændset]	Fernbedienung
sight	['saɪt]	Sicht
eject	[i'dʒekt]	auswerfen
tape counter	['teɪp kaʊntə]	Bandzähler
display	[dɪ'spleɪ]	Anzeige
panel	['pænl]	Feld, Tafel
current	['kʌrənt]	augenblicklich, aktuell
clear	[klɪə]	auf Null stellen
reset	[ˌriː'set]	zurückstellen
zero	['zɪərəʊ]	Null
rewind	[ˌriː'waɪnd]	zurückspulen
playback picture	['pleɪbæk pɪktʃə]	Playbackbild
switch to	['swɪtʃ tə]	umschalten auf
still picture	[ˌstɪl 'pɪktʃə]	Standbild
select	[sɪ'lekt]	auswählen
channel	['tʃænl]	Kanal
child lock	['tʃaɪld lɒk]	Kindersicherung
wind forward	[ˌwaɪnd 'fɔːwəd]	vorlaufen
quick set recording	[ˌkwɪk set rɪ'kɔːdɪŋ]	Aufnahme

49p
insert	[ɪn'sɜːt]	einlegen
make sure	[ˌmeɪk 'ʃʊə]	sich vergewissern
position	[pə'zɪʃn]	Position
section	['sekʃn]	Abschnitt

Unit 7

50
beauty	['bjuːti]	Schönheit
day cream	['deɪ kriːm]	Tagescreme
sensitive	['sensətɪv]	empfindlich, sensibel
skin	[skɪn]	Haut
for instance	[fə'rɪnstəns]	zum Beispiel
range	[reɪndʒ]	Sortiment
tester	['testə]	Probe
natural	['nætʃrəl]	natürlich
medicine	['medsn]	Medikament(e)
alternative	[ɔːl'tɜːnətɪv]	Alternative
brochure	['brəʊʃə]	Broschüre
Anti-Vivisection Campaign	[ˌænti vɪvɪˌsekʃn kæm'peɪn]	Aktion gegen Tierversuche

51
look at	['lʊk ət]	ansehen
pamphlet	['pæmflət]	Broschüre
against	[ə'genst]	gegen
animal testing	['ænɪml testɪŋ]	Tierversuche
stuff	[stʌf]	Zeug
human	['hjuːmən]	Mensch
cruel	[kruːəl]	grausam
creature	['kriːtʃə]	Geschöpf

guinea-pig	['gɪnipɪg]	Versuchskaninchen
as well	[əz 'wel]	auch (noch), ebenfalls
cause	[kɔːz]	verursachen, auslösen
allergy	['ælədʒi]	Allergie
rabbit	['ræbɪt]	Kaninchen
prove safe	[pruːv 'seɪf]	sich als sicher erweisen
in vitro	[ɪn 'viːtrəʊ]	im Reagenzglas
involve	[ɪn'vɒlv]	einschließen, umfassen

52
argument	['ɑːgjumənt]	Argument
as far as	[əz 'fɑːr əz]	so weit
suppose	[sə'pəʊz]	glauben, vermuten, denken
on the one hand	[ɒn ðə 'wʌn hænd]	einerseits
on the other hand	[ɒn ði 'ʌðə hænd]	andererseits

54
skincare product	[ˌskɪnkeə 'prɒdʌkt]	Hautpflegeprodukt
formulate	['fɔːmjuleɪt]	formulieren
analyze	['ænəlaɪz]	analysieren
skin type	['skɪn taɪp]	Hauttyp
characteristic	[ˌkærəktə'rɪstɪk]	typisches Merkmal
irritate	['ɪrɪteɪt]	reizen
oily	['ɔɪli]	fettig
T-zone	['tiː zəʊn]	T-Bereich
slightly	['slaɪtli]	leicht
blemished	['blemɪʃt]	picklig
frequent	['friːkwənt]	häufig
breakout	['breɪkaʊt]	Entzündung
basics	['beɪsɪks]	Grundregeln
teen	[tiːn]	Teenager
cleanser	['klenzə]	Reiniger
overdry	[ˌəʊvə'draɪ]	austrocknen
preferably	['prefərəbli]	vorzugsweise
pollution	[pə'luːʃn]	Verschmutzung
remain	[rɪ'meɪn]	bleiben
active	['æktɪv]	aktiv, tätig
moisturizer	['mɔɪstʃəraɪzə]	Feuchtigkeitscreme
oil-free	[ˌɔɪl 'friː]	fettfrei
blemish	['blemɪʃ]	Pickellotion
cotton wool bud	[ˌkɒtn'wʊl bʌd]	Wattebausch
face mask	['feɪs mɑːsk]	Gesichtsmaske
balance	['bæləns]	ausgleichen
tighten	['taɪtn]	festigen
pore	[pɔː]	Pore
apply	[ə'plaɪ]	anlegen
scrub	[skrʌb]	Gesichtspeeling
gentle	['dʒentl]	sanft
complexion	[kəm'plekʃn]	Teint
spot	[spɒt]	Pickel
grain	[greɪn]	Grain
rinse off	[ˌrɪns 'ɒf]	abspülen
fight	[faɪt]	bekämpfen
blackhead	['blækhed]	Mitesser

55
secret	['siːkrɪt]	Geheimnis
spill	[spɪl]	verschütten

55t
ingredients	[ɪn'griːdiənts]	Zutaten
beat	[biːt]	schlagen
teaspoon	['tiːspuːn]	Teelöffel

olive oil [ˌɒlɪv ˈɔɪl]	Olivenöl
sea salt [ˈsiː sɔːlt]	Meersalz
whole milk [ˌhəʊl ˈmɪlk]	Vollmilch
thorough [ˈθʌrə]	gründlich
spread [spred]	streichen, verteilen
leave on [ˌliːv ˈɒn]	darauf lassen
rinse [rɪns]	spülen

55
fortunately [ˈfɔːtʃənətli]	glücklicherweise

56
injured [ˈɪndʒəd]	verletzt
career [kəˈrɪə]	Karriere
opposite [ˈɒpəzɪt]	Gegenteil
resistant [rɪˈzɪstənt]	strapazierfähig
artificial [ˌɑːtɪˈfɪʃl]	künstlich
odd [ɒd]	nicht passend
curler [ˈkɜːlə]	Lockenwickler
comb [kəʊm]	Kamm
razor [ˈreɪzə]	Rasierer
scissors [ˈsɪsəz]	Schere
eyeshadow [ˈaɪʃædəʊ]	Lidschatten
lipstick [ˈlɪpstɪk]	Lippenstift
sunblock [ˈsʌnblɒk]	Sonnenschutz

Unit 8

57
mercury [ˈmɜːkjəri]	Quecksilber
recharge [ˌriːˈtʃɑːdʒ]	aufladen
can [kæn]	Dose
recycle [ˌriːˈsaɪkl]	recyceln
public transport [ˌpʌblɪk ˈtrænspɔːt]	öffentliche Verkehrsmittel
aerosol [ˈeərəsɒl]	Spraydose
toiletries [ˈtɔɪlətriz]	Toilettenartikel
unnecessary [ʌnˈnesəsri]	unnötig
wrapping [ˈræpɪŋ]	Verpackung
chlorofluorocarbon blown [ˌklɔːrəʊˌflʊərəʊˈkɑːbən bləʊn]	FCK-Schaumstoff
polystyrene foam [ˌpɒliˈstaɪriːn fəʊm]	Polystyrol, Styropor
fast food [ˌfɑːst ˈfuːd]	Schnellgerichte

58
process [ˈprəʊses]	(weiter)verarbeiten
fertilizer [ˈfɜːtəlaɪzə]	Dünger
pesticide [ˈpestɪsaɪd]	Pestizid
prove [pruːv]	beweisen
farmer [ˈfɑːmə]	Bauer, Bäuerin
organization [ˌɔːɡənaɪˈzeɪʃn]	Organisation
certify [ˈsɜːtɪfaɪ]	beglaubigen
strict [strɪkt]	streng
soil [sɔɪl]	Erde
remains [rɪˈmeɪnz]	Rückstände
field [fiːld]	Feld
inspect [ɪnˈspekt]	inspizieren
forbidden [fəˈbɪdn]	verboten
substance [ˈsʌbstəns]	Substanz, Stoff
hen [hen]	Huhn
lock up [ˌlɒk ˈʌp]	einsperren
cage [keɪdʒ]	Käfig
condition [kənˈdɪʃn]	Bedingung
space [speɪs]	Raum
run around [ˌrʌn əˈraʊnd]	herumrennen
square metre [ˈskweə miːtə]	Quadratmeter
cow [kaʊ]	Kuh

be allowed to [bi əˈlaʊd tə]	dürfen

59
cheating [ˈtʃiːtɪŋ]	Betrug
honest [ˈɒnɪst]	ehrlich
majority [məˈdʒɒrəti]	Mehrheit
claim [kleɪm]	behaupten
conventional [kənˈvenʃənl]	konventionell
left over [left ˈəʊvə]	übrig geblieben
chemical [ˈkemɪkl]	chemisch
kill [kɪl]	töten, umbringen
weeds [wiːdz]	Unkraut
insect [ˈɪnsekt]	Insekt
truth [truːθ]	Wahrheit
minority [maɪˈnɒrəti]	Minderheit

60
GE [ˌdʒiː ˈiː]	Gentechnik
nature [ˈneɪtʃə]	Natur
gene [dʒiːn]	Gen
clump [klʌmp]	Klumpen
cell [sel]	Zelle
genetic code [dʒəˌnetɪk ˈkəʊd]	genetischer Code
divide [dɪˈvaɪd]	(sich) teilen
mutation [mjuːˈteɪʃn]	Mutation
business [ˈbɪznəs]	Geschäft
evolution [ˌiːvəˈluːʃn]	Evolution
point [pɔɪnt]	Sinn
mess around with [ˌmes əˈbaʊt wɪð]	herumpfuschen
impatient [ɪmˈpeɪʃnt]	ungeduldig
organism [ˈɔːɡənɪzəm]	Organismus
ability [əˈbɪləti]	Fähigkeit
resist [rɪˈzɪst]	widerstehen
disease [dɪˈziːz]	Krankheit, Erkrankung
scientist [ˈsaɪəntɪst]	(Natur-)Wissenschaftler/in
programme [ˈprəʊɡræm]	programmieren
produce [prəˈdjuːs]	produzieren
vaccine [ˈvæksiːn]	Impfstoff
illness [ˈɪlnəs]	Krankheit
risky [ˈrɪski]	riskant
nor [nɔː]	auch nicht, noch
effect [ɪˈfekt]	(Aus-)Wirkung
starve [stɑːv]	(ver)hungern

61
comprehension [ˌkɒmprɪˈhenʃn]	Verständnis
side effect [ˈsaɪd ɪfekt]	Nebenwirkung
silly [ˈsɪli]	töricht
profit [ˈprɒfɪt]	Profit

62
synonym [ˈsɪnənɪm]	Synonym
veggie [ˌɡəʊɪŋ ˈvedʒi]	Vegetarier/in

62p
vegetarian [ˌvedʒəˈteəriən]	Vegetarier/in
disgusting [dɪsˈɡʌstɪŋ]	ekelhaft
flesh [fleʃ]	Fleisch
raise [reɪz]	aufziehen
protein [ˈprəʊtiːn]	Protein
non-meat [ˌnɒn ˈmiːt]	fleischlos
hypocritical [ˌhɪpəˈkrɪtɪkl]	heuchlerisch
avoid [əˈvɔɪd]	vermeiden
whenever [wenˈevə]	immer wenn
awkward [ˈɔːkwəd]	ungeschickt
invite [ɪnˈvaɪt]	einladen

63

patient	['peɪʃnt]	geduldig
fair	[feə]	fair, gerecht
mature	[məˈtʃʊə]	reif
smoker	[ˈsməʊkə]	Raucher/in
responsible	[rɪˈspɒnsəbl]	verantwortlich
logical	[ˈlɒdʒɪkl]	logisch
employ	[ɪmˈplɔɪ]	beschäftigen
friendly	[ˈfrendli]	freundlich
independent	[ˌɪndɪˈpendənt]	unabhängig
real	[rɪəl]	echt, wirklich
pessimism	[ˈpesɪmɪzəm]	Pessimismus
reason	[ˈriːzn]	Vernunft, Grund
sense	[sens]	Sinn, Gefühl, Empfindung
tradition	[trəˈdɪʃn]	Tradition

Unit 9

64

bracelet	[ˈbreɪslət]	Armband, -reif
necklace	[ˈnekləs]	(Hals-)Kette
chain	[ˈtʃeɪn]	Kette
pendant	[ˈpendənt]	Anhänger
gemstone	[ˈdʒemstəʊn]	Edelstein
pierce	[pɪəs]	lochen
carat	[ˈkærət]	Karat
gold-plated	[ˌɡəʊld ˈpleɪtɪd]	vergoldet
sterling silver	[ˌstɜːlɪŋ ˈsɪlvə]	Sterlingsilber
fashion	[ˈfæʃn]	Mode
hypo-allergenic	[ˌhaɪpəʊ ˌæləˈdʒenɪk]	anti-allergische

65

bangle	[ˈbæŋɡl]	Armreif
brooch	[brəʊtʃ]	Brosche
pin	[pɪn]	(Ansteck-)Nadel
cuff links	[ˈkʌflɪŋks]	Manschettenknöpfe
hoop earrings	[huːp ˈɪərɪŋz]	Ohrreifen
pearl	[pɜːl]	Perle
stud earrings	[stʌd ˈɪərɪŋz]	Ohrstecker
tie clip	[ˈtaɪ klɪp]	Krawattenspange
wedding ring	[ˈwedɪŋ rɪŋ]	Ehering
watchmaker	[ˈwɒtʃmeɪkə]	Uhrmacher/in
water-resistant	[ˈwɔːtə rɪzɪstənt]	wasserdicht
dive	[daɪv]	tauchen
inexpensive	[ˌɪnɪkˈspensɪv]	preiswert

67

set	[set]	(ein)stellen
winder	[ˈwaɪndə]	Aufzugsknopf
click	[klɪk]	Klicken
clockface	[klɑːk]	Zifferblatt
lapis lazuli	[ˌlæpɪs ˈlæzjuli]	Lapislazuli
hematite	[ˈhemətaɪt]	Hämatit
topaz	[ˈtəʊpæz]	Topas
jasper	[ˈdʒæspə]	Jaspis
amber	[ˈæmbə]	Bernstein
garnet	[ˈɡɑːnɪt]	Granat
emerald	[ˈemərəld]	Smaragd
rock crystal	[ˈrɒk krɪstl]	Bergkristall
opal	[ˈəʊpl]	Opal
ruby	[ˈruːbi]	Rubin
sapphire	[ˈsæfaɪə]	Saphir

67p

creativity	[ˌkriːeɪˈtɪvəti]	Kreativität
happiness	[ˈhæpɪnəs]	Glück, Fröhlichkeit
joy	[dʒɔɪ]	Freude
intensify	[ɪnˈtensɪfaɪ]	verstärken
sexual	[ˈsekʃuəl]	sexuell
attraction	[əˈtrækʃn]	Anziehung
logic	[ˈlɒdʒɪk]	Logik
dispute	[dɪˈspjuːt]	Auseinandersetzung
transparent	[trænsˈpærənt]	durchsichtig
primarily	[praɪˈmerəli]	vor allem, hauptsächlich
foretell	[fɔːˈtel]	vorhersagen
future	[ˈfjuːtʃə]	Zukunft
crystal balls	[ˌkrɪstl ˈbɔːlz]	Kristallkugeln
luck	[lʌk]	Glück
spiritual	[ˈspɪrɪtʃuəl]	geistig
calm	[kɑːm]	Ruhe
deal, a great ~ of	[ə ɡreɪt diːl əv]	eine Menge von
purify	[ˈpjʊərɪfaɪ]	reinigen
thought	[θɔːt]	Gedanke
wisdom	[ˈwɪzdəm]	Weisheit
suppress	[səˈpres]	unterdrücken
envy	[ˈenvi]	Neid
vitality	[vaɪˈtæləti]	Vitalität
improve	[ɪmˈpruːv]	verbessern
appetite	[ˈæpɪtaɪt]	Appetit
weight	[weɪt]	Gewicht
ward off	[ˌwɔːd ˈɒf]	abwehren
disaster	[dɪˈzɑːstə]	Katastrophe
blessing	[ˈblesɪŋ]	Segen
recipient	[rɪˈsɪpiənt]	Empfänger/in

68

throughout	[θruːˈaʊt]	überall (in), die ganze Zeit hindurch
history	[ˈhɪstri]	Geschichte
heal	[hiːl]	heilen
precious	[ˈpreʃəs]	Edel-
semi-precious	[ˌsemiˈpreʃəs]	Halbedel-
tension	[ˈtenʃn]	Spannung
ease	[iːz]	lindern
anklet	[ˈæŋklət]	Fußkettchen
barrier	[ˈbæriə]	Schranke
joyful	[ˈdʒɔɪfl]	freudig
lack	[læk]	mangeln an
confidence	[ˈkɒnfɪdəns]	Selbstvertrauen
influence	[ˈɪnfluəns]	beeinflussen
imagination	[ɪˌmædʒɪˈneɪʃn]	Vorstellungskraft
bearer	[ˈbeərə]	Träger/in
neutralize	[ˈnjuːtrəlaɪz]	neutralisieren
fear	[fɪə]	Angst, Befürchtung
weakness	[ˈwiːknəs]	Schwäche
emotion	[ɪˈməʊʃn]	Gefühl
resistance	[rɪˈzɪstəns]	Widerstand
rational	[ˈræʃnəl]	rational
intuition	[ˌɪntjuˈɪʃn]	Intuition
determination	[dɪˌtɜːmɪˈneɪʃn]	Entschlossenheit
symbolize	[ˈsɪmbəlaɪz]	symbolisieren
patience	[ˈpeɪʃns]	Geduld
tolerance	[ˈtɒlərəns]	Toleranz
powerful	[ˈpaʊəfl]	stark
ancient	[ˈeɪnʃənt]	alt
meditation	[ˌmedɪˈteɪʃn]	Meditation
stressed	[strest]	gestresst
inner	[ˈɪnə]	innere(r,s)
jealous	[ˈdʒeləs]	eifersüchtig

69

burglary	[ˈbɜːɡləri]	Einbruch

69t

supper ['sʌpə]	(das) Abendessen
suddenly ['sʌdnli]	plötzlich
hear [hɪə]	hören
wake up [ˌweɪk 'ʌp]	aufwachen
telly ['teli]	Fernseher
alarm [ə'lɑ:m]	Alarm(anlage)
go off [ˌgəʊ 'ɒf]	losgehen
scream [skri:m]	Schrei
past [pɑ:st]	an ... vorbei

70

witness ['wɪtnəs]	Zeuge, Zeugin
policeman [pə'li:smən]	Polizist
crime [kraɪm]	Verbrechen

Unit 10

71

DIY store [ˌdi: aɪ 'waɪ stɔ:]	Bau-, Heimwerkermarkt
hammer/rotary drill ['hæmə, 'rəʊtəri drɪl]	Schlagbohrer
masonry bit ['meɪsənri bɪt]	Betonbohrer
depth gauge ['depθ geɪdʒ]	Tiefenmesser
rubber backing pad [ˌrʌbə 'bækɪŋ pæd]	Gummipolster
sanding disc ['sændɪŋ dɪsk]	Schmirgelscheibe
wall plug ['wɔ:l plʌg]	Dübel
jigsaw ['dʒɪgsɔ:]	Stichsäge
adjustable [ə'dʒʌstəbl]	verstellbar
baseplate ['beɪspleɪt]	Grund-, Sockelplatte
shield [ʃi:ld]	(Schutz-)Schild
fork [fɔ:k]	Gabel
spade [speɪd]	Spaten
carbon steel [ˌkɑ:bən 'sti:l]	Kohlenstoffstahl
petrol mower ['petrəl məʊə]	Benzinmäher
lead [li:d]	Hundeleine
one-handed [ˌwʌn'hændɪd]	Einhand-
control trigger [kən'trəʊl trɪgə]	Trigger
act as ['ækt əz]	dienen als
approximately [ə'prɒksɪmətli]	zirka
pressure washer ['preʃə wɒʃə]	Hochdruckreiniger
volume ['vɒlju:m]	Volumen, Menge
supply [sə'plaɪ]	liefern
hose [həʊz]	Schlauch
lance [lɑ:ns]	Lanze
tool kit ['tu:l kɪt]	Werkzeugkasten
basic ['beɪsɪk]	elementar
general ['dʒenrəl]	allgemein
carpentry ['kɑ:pəntri]	Tischlerarbeiten
kettle barbecue [ˌketl 'bɑ:bɪkju:]	Grillgerät
enamelled [ɪ'næmld]	emailliert
chrome [krəʊm]	Chrom
cooking grid ['kʊkɪŋ grɪd]	Rost
mobility [məʊ'bɪləti]	Beweglichkeit
wire ['waɪə]	Draht

72

revolution [ˌrevə'lu:ʃn]	Umdrehung

72t

screwdriver ['skru:draɪvə]	Schraubenzieher
rope [rəʊp]	Seil

72

power drill ['paʊə drɪl]	Elektrobohrer
corded ['kɔ:dɪd]	mit Kabel
cordless ['kɔ:dləs]	kabellos
mains power ['meɪnz paʊə]	Stromnetz
ladder ['lædə]	Leiter
concrete ['kɒŋkri:t]	Beton
vibrate ['vaɪbreɪt]	vibrieren
masonry ['meɪsənri]	Mauerwerk
wattage ['wɒtɪdʒ]	Wattleistung

75

society [sə'saɪəti]	Gesellschaft
shift ['ʃɪft]	Schicht
time, take up ~ [ˌteɪk 'ʌp taɪm]	Zeit verbrauchen
sort [sɔ:t]	Art
frequently ['fri:kwəntli]	häufig
smelly ['smeli]	stinkend
endless ['endləs]	endlos
attention span [ə'tenʃn spæn]	Aufmerksamkeitsspanne
common sense [ˌkɒmən 'sens]	gesunder Menschenverstand
duty ['dju:ti]	Pflicht
forgetful [fə'getfl]	vergesslich
commitment [kə'mɪtmənt]	Verpflichtung
responsibility [rɪˌspɒnsə'bɪləti]	Verantwortung
fairly ['feəli]	ziemlich
self-sufficient [ˌself sə'fɪʃənt]	autark
virtual ['vɜ:tʃuəl]	virtuell
own [əʊn]	besitzen

76

vet(erinarian) [vet] [ˌvetərɪneəriən]	Tierarzt, -ärztin
exotic [ɪg'zɒtɪk]	exotisch

76t

lonely ['ləʊnli]	einsam
tolerant ['tɒlərənt]	tolerant
period ['pɪəriəd]	Zeit(raum), Zeitspanne
litter-box ['lɪtəbɒks]	Katzenklo
allergic [ə'lɜ:dʒɪk]	allergisch
reaction [ri'ækʃn]	Reaktion
walk, take a ~ [ˌteɪk ə 'wɔ:k]	spazieren gehen
companion [kəm'pæniən]	Begleiter/in
vaccination [ˌvæksɪ'neɪʃn]	Impfung
medical ['medɪkl]	medizinisch
insurance [ɪn'ʃʊərəns]	Versicherung
snake [sneɪk]	Schlange
lizard ['lɪzəd]	Eidechse
import [ɪm'pɔ:t]	importieren
overseas [ˌəʊvə'si:z]	Übersee
parrot ['pærət]	Papagei
turtle ['tɜ:tl]	Wasserschildkröte
survive [sə'vaɪv]	überleben
journey ['dʒɜ:ni]	Reise
bark [bɑ:k]	bellen
enormous [ɪ'nɔ:məs]	enorm

76

scratchpost ['skrætʃpəʊst]	Kratzbaum
cathouse ['kæthaʊs]	Katzentransportkäfig
feeding bowl ['fi:dɪŋ bəʊl]	Futternapf
muzzle ['mʌzl]	Maulkorb
sleeping basket ['sli:pɪŋ bɑ:skɪt]	Schlafkörbchen

Unit 11

77
gun [gʌn]		Pistole
laser pistol ['leɪzə pɪstl]		Laserpistole
space invader [ˌspeɪs ɪn'veɪdə]		Angreifer aus dem Weltall
war game ['wɔːgeɪm]		Kriegsspiel
industry ['ɪndəstri]		Industrie
advertising ['ædvətaɪzɪŋ]		Werbung
monster ['mɒnstə]		Monster
technical ['teknɪkl]		technisch
violent ['vaɪələnt]		gewalttätig
racing car ['reɪsɪŋ kɑː]		Rennwagen

78
off-roader [ˌɒf 'rəʊdə]		Geländewagen
fact ['fækt]		Faktum
zebra ['zebrə]		Zebra
vehicle ['viːəkl]		Fahrzeug
explorer [ɪk'splɔːrə]		Forscher/in
toucan [pet 'tuːkæn]		Tukan
container [kən'teɪnə]		Behälter
sheep [ʃiːp]		Schaf
colourful ['kʌləfl]		bunt, farbig
bead [biːd]		Perle
number ['nʌmbə]		Ziffer, Zahl
twinkling ['twɪŋklɪŋ]		glitzernd, flimmernd
stimulate ['stɪmjuleɪt]		anregen
combination [ˌkɒmbɪ'neɪʃn]		Kombination
puzzling ['pʌzlɪŋ]		Puzzlespiel
modelling ['mɒdlɪŋ]		Modellbau
typical ['tɪpɪkl]		typisch
tourist attraction [ˌtʊərɪst ə'trækʃn]		Touristenattraktion
bear [beə]		Bär
squeeze [skwiːz]		drücken
toddler ['tɒdlə]		Kleinkind
back and forth [ˌbæk ənd 'fɔːθ]		vor und zurück
cloth [klɒθ]		Stoff
exciting [ɪk'saɪtɪŋ]		spannend
hand-held ['hændheld]		tragbar
entertain [ˌentə'teɪn]		unterhalten
coordination [kəʊˌɔːdɪ'neɪʃn]		Koordination
doll's house ['dɒlz haʊs]		Puppenstube
furnish ['fɜːnɪʃ]		möblieren
fold up [ˌfəʊld 'ʌp]		zusammenklappen
sturdy ['stɜːdi]		stabil
plastic ['plæstɪk]		Plastik
mains transformer [ˌmeɪnz træns'fɔːmə]		Stromtransformator
headlights ['hedlaɪts]		Scheinwerfer
magnetic [mæg'netɪk]		magnetisch
controller [kən'trəʊlə]		Fernlenker
track [træk]		Rennstrecke

79
excluded [ɪk'skluːdɪd]		ausgeschlossen

80
batteries, run on ~ [ˌrʌn ɒn 'bætəriz]		batteriebetrieben

81
shoplifter ['ʃɒplɪftə]		Ladendieb(in)
shove [ʃʌv]		stoßen
crowd [kraʊd]		Menschenmenge
reach [riːtʃ]		erreichen
detective [dɪ'tektɪv]		Detektiv-
biro ['baɪrəʊ]		Kugelschreiber
tears, in ~ [ɪn tɪəz]		in Tränen aufgelöst
cashier [kæ'ʃɪə]		Kassierer(in)
video game [vɪdiəʊ geɪm]		Computerspiel
thief [θiːf]		Dieb/in
stupid ['stjuːpɪd]		dumm
prosecute ['prɒsɪkjuːt]		strafrechtlich verfolgen
prison ['prɪzn]		Gefängnis
fine [faɪn]		Geldstrafe

82
out of stock [aʊt əv 'stɒk]		nicht vorrätig
homonym ['hɒmənɪm]		Homonym
bow [bəʊ]		Schleife
bow down [ˌbaʊ 'daʊn]		sich verbeugen

83
bench [bentʃ]		Bank, Sitzbank
goal [gəʊl]		Tor
fool [fuːl]		Narr/Närrin
gate [geɪt]		Tor, Pforte
sheet [ʃiːt]		Blatt (Papier)
leaf [liːf]		Blatt
blanket ['blæŋkɪt]		(Woll-)Decke
ceiling ['siːlɪŋ]		(Zimmer-)Decke
paragraph ['pærəgrɑːf]		Absatz, Abschnitt
landing ['lændɪŋ]		Gang (im oberen Stock)
spring [sprɪŋ]		(Sprung-)Feder
feather ['feðə]		Feder
nib [nɪb]		(Schreib-)Feder
prescription [prɪ'skrɪpʃn]		Rezept
tear [teə]		zerreißen
bare [beə]		nackt, bloß
fare [feə]		Flug-, Fahrpreis
peace [piːs]		Frieden

Unit 12

84
job centre ['dʒɒbsentə]		Arbeitsamt
kid [kɪd]		Kind
communicate [kə'mjuːnɪkeɪt]		sich verständigen
wage [weɪdʒ]		Lohn
staff [stɑːf]		Mitarbeiter/innen
sweaty feet [sweti fiːt]		Schweißfüße

85
retailing ['riːteɪlɪŋ]		Einzelhandel
catch up with [ˌkætʃ 'ʌp wɪð]		treffen
advert ['ædvɜːt]		Anzeige
basic knowledge [ˌbeɪsɪk 'nɒlɪdʒ]		Grundkenntnisse
mobile phone stall [ˌməʊbaɪl 'fəʊn stɔːl]		Stand für Mobilfunk
trial period [ˌtraɪəl 'pɪəriəd]		Probezeit
be familiar with [bi fə'mɪliə wɪð]		sich gut auskennen mit
discount ['dɪskaʊnt]		Rabatt
drag [dræg]		Belastung
definition [ˌdefɪ'nɪʃn]		Definition
employee [ɪm'plɔɪiː]		Angestellte/r
work overtime [ˌwɜːk 'əʊvətaɪm]		Überstunden machen

weekly ['wiːkli]	wöchentlich	92	
manual work [ˌmænjuəl 'wɜːk]	Handarbeit	state [steɪt]	angeben
		line space ['laɪn speɪs]	Leerzeile
employer [ɪm'plɔɪə]	Arbeitgeber/in	regards, with best ~ [wɪð ˌbest rɪ'gɑːdz]	Viele Grüße
salary ['sæləri]	Gehalt, Lohn	invoice ['ɪnvɔɪs]	Rechnung
86		public limited company [ˌpʌblɪk ˌlɪmɪtɪd 'kʌmpəni]	Aktiengesellschaft
vacant ['veɪkənt]	frei		
rise [raɪz]	(Gehalts-)Erhöhung	for the attention of [fə ði ə'tenʃn əv]	zu Händen von
personnel manager [pɜːsə'nel mænɪdʒə]	Personalchef/in	93	
88		warehouse ['weəhaʊs]	Lagerhaus
part-time [ˌpɑːt'taɪm]	Teilzeit-	incomplete [ˌɪnkəm'pliːt]	unvollständig
expand [ɪk'spænd]	expandieren, vergrößern	94	
ambitious [æm'bɪʃəs]	ehrgeizig	voicemail ['vɔɪsmeɪl]	Mailbox
selling ['selɪŋ]	Verkauf	94t	
fluent ['fluːənt]	fließend	crash [kræʃ]	abstürzen
curriculum vitae [kəˌrɪkjələm 'viːtaɪ]	Lebenslauf	strike [straɪk]	Streik
88t		94	
quite a few [kwaɪt ə 'fjuː]	eine ganze Menge	finalize ['faɪnəlaɪz]	endgültig festlegen
caller ['kɔːlə]	Anrufer/in	safety [ˌseɪfti]	Sicherheit
close down [ˌkləʊz 'daʊn]	schließen	payment ['peɪmənt]	Bezahlung
settle in [ˌsetl 'ɪn]	sich zurechtfinden	95	
90		tab [tæb]	Feld
education [ˌedʒu'keɪʃn]	Ausbildung	keyword ['kiːwɜːd]	Stichwort
job experience [ˌdʒɒb ɪk'spɪəriəns]	Berufserfahrung	browse [braʊz]	durchsehen
		category ['kætəgəri]	Kategorie
90p		listing ['lɪstɪŋ]	Eintrag
primary school ['praɪməri skuːl]	Grundschule	click on ['klɪk ɒn]	klicken auf
secondary school ['sekəndri skuːl]	weiterführende Schule	shopping cart ['ʃɒpɪŋ kɑːt]	Einkaufswagen
		proceed [prə'siːd]	weitergehen
		check out [ˌtʃek 'aʊt]	hinausgehen
90		delete [dɪ'liːt]	löschen
neither ['naɪðə]	keiner	icon ['aɪkɒn]	Symbol
applicant ['æplɪkənt]	Bewerber/in	opportunity [ˌɒpə'tjuːnəti]	Gelegenheit
91		shipping ['ʃɪpɪŋ]	Versand
(carbon) copies [ˌkɑːbən 'kɒpiz]	Kopien	option ['ɒpʃn]	Option
body of the letter [ˌbɒdi əv ðə 'letə]	Hauptteil des Briefes	purchase ['pɜːtʃəs]	(Ein-)Kauf
		transaction [træn'zækʃn]	Geschäft
		unauthorized [ˌʌn'ɔːθəraɪzd]	unbefugt
enclosure [ɪn'kləʊʒə]	Anlage	digit ['dɪdʒɪt]	Ziffer
subject line ['sʌbdʒɪkt laɪn]	Betreffzeile	submit [səb'mɪt]	unterbreiten
		prompt [prɒmpt]	auffordern

A–Z word list

Diese Liste enthällt alle Wörter in alphabetischer Reihenfolge. Es sind jedoch die Wörter, die zum Grundwortschatz gehören, hier nicht aufgeführt. (Siehe *Basic Word List*)

p = das Wort befindet sich im *pairwork file*.
t = das Wort befindet sich im *transcript*.

A

a little *21t* ein wenig, ein bisschen
ability *60* Fähigkeit
able, to be ~ to *41* können
accident *36* Unfall
according to *23* entsprechend
account for *47* ausmachen
act as *71* dienen als
active *54* aktiv, tätig
activity *13* Aktivität, Tätigkeit
additional *45* zusätzlich
adequate *35* ausreichend
adjustable *71* verstellbar
advantage *14* Vorzug
adventure *21t* Abenteuer
advert *85* Anzeige
advertise *19* werben (für)
advertising *77* Werbung
aerial *29* Antenne
aerobics *18* Aerobik
aerosol *57* Spraydose
afford *21t* sich leisten (können)
against *51* gegen
ahead of *16* vor
aid *16* helfen
alarm *69t* Alarm(anlage)
allergic *76t* allergisch
allergy *51* Allergie
allowed to, be ~ *58* dürfen
almost *40* fast, beinahe
alone *44* allein(e)
Alps, the ~ *21t* die Alpen
alter *31* ändern
alternative *50* Alternative
although *24* obwohl
amber *67* Bernstein
ambitious *88* ehrgeizig
analyze *54* analysieren
ancient *68* alt
animal testing *51* Tierversuche
ankle boot *8* Halbstiefel
ankle collar *8* Schaftrand
anklet *68* Fußkettchen

anti-flood system *45* Überlaufschutz
Anti-Vivisection Campaign *50* Aktion gegen Tierversuche
anxiety *14* Angst(zustand)
appetite *67p* Appetit
applicant *90* Bewerber/in
apply to *13* gelten/zutreffen für
apply *54* anlegen
appropriate *18* geeignet, angemessen, passend
approximately *71* zirka
area *23* Bereich
argument *52* Argument
around here *24* hier herum
artificial *56* künstlich
as far as *52* so weit
as soon as *37t* sobald
as well *51* auch (noch), ebenfalls
ash *35* Esche
at a glance *47* auf einen Blick
at all *13* überhaupt
at home *13* zu Hause
at least *13* wenigstens, mindestens
at the same time *24* gleichzeitig
at the seaside *26* am Meer
at work *14* bei der Arbeit
attach *24* anbringen
attachment *40* Aufsatz
attend *21t* teilnehmen an, besuchen
attention span *75* Aufmerksamkeitsspanne
attention, for the ~ of *92* zu Händen von
attraction *67p* Anziehung
average *47* durchschnittlich
avoid *62p* vermeiden
aware, be ~ *44* sich bewusst sein
awful *24* furchtbar, schrecklich
awkward *62p* ungeschickt

B

back and forth *78* vor und zurück
back *16* Rücken
balance *54* ausgleichen
balanced *14* ausgewogen
balcony *28* Balkon
bangle *65* Armreif
bare *83* nackt, bloß
bargain *6* günstiges Angebot
bark *76t* bellen
barrier *68* Schranke
base *40* Fuß
based on, be ~ *47* basieren auf

baseplate *71* Grund-, Sockelplatte
basic knowledge *85* Grundkenntnisse
basic *71* elementar
basics *54* Grundregeln
basis *44* Basis
bathroom *28* Badezimmer
batteries, run on ~ *80* batteriebetrieben
bay window *29* Erkerfenster
bead *78* Perle
bear *78* Bär
bearer *68* Träger/in
beat *55t* schlagen
beauty *50* Schönheit
bedroom *28* Schlafzimmer
begin, to ~ with *23* zunächst, anfangs
beige *6* beige
bell *25* Klingel
bench *83* Bank, Sitzbank
bicycle, bike *24* Fahrrad
biker *24* Radfahrer/in
binding *11* Bindung
biro *81* Kugelschreiber
blackhead *54* Mitesser
blade *40* Klinge
blanket *83* (Woll-)Decke
blemish *54* Pickel
blemished *54* picklig
blend *35* Mischung, Gemisch
blender *40* Mischer, Mixer
blessing *67p* Segen
blood pressure *18* Blutdruck
blood *16* Blut
body of the letter *91* Hauptteil des Briefes
body, part of the ~ *16* Körperteil
bone *18* Knochen
bookshelf *30* (Bücher-)Regal
boost *16* erhöhen, verstärken
boot *7* Stiefel
boring *6* langweilig
bottom *16* Hintern
bottoms *19* Hose
bow down *82* sich verbeugen
bow *82* Schleife
bracelet *64* Armband, -reif
brain *16* Gehirn
brake *25* Bremse
break down *47* versagen
breakout *54* Entzündung
breathless *18* außer Atem
brisk *18* lebhaft, kräftig
brochure *50* Broschüre

brooch 65 Brosche
browning control 40 Bräunungsregler
browse 95 durchsehen
buckle 8 Schnalle
build up 16 steigern
build 18 (auf)bauen
bulb 44 Glühbirne
burglary 69 Einbruch
burn 18 verbrennen
business 60 Geschäft
by hand 46 mit der Hand
by phone 38 telefonisch
by the way 28t übrigens, nebenbei

C

cage 58 Käfig
calf 16 Wade
caller 18 Anrufer/in
calm 67p Ruhe
calorie 18 Kalorie
can 57 Dose
canvas 8 Segeltuch
capacity 38 Fassungsvermögen
car park 25 Parkplatz
carat 64 Karat
(carbon) copies 91 Kopien
carbon steel 71 Kohlenstoffstahl
care about 14 sich kümmern um
care instructions 19 Pflegeanleitung
career 56 Karriere
carpentry 71 Tischlerarbeiten
carriage 40 Schlitten
cash desk 19 Kasse
cashier 81 Kassierer(in)
catch up with 85 treffen
category 95 Kategorie
cathouse 76 Katzentransportkäfig
cause 51 verursachen, auslösen
ceiling 83 (Zimmer-)Decke
cell 60 Zelle
central heating 28 Zentralheizung
certify 58 beglaubigen
chain cover 25 Kettenschutz
chain 64 Kette
challenge 23 Herausforderung
chance 23 Chance, Gelegenheit
channel 49 Kanal
characteristic 54 typisches Merkmal
charge 38 Kosten, Gebühr; 38t berechnen
cheating 59 Betrug
check out 95 hinausgehen
chemical 59 chemisch
chenille 35 Chenille
cheque 38 Scheck
cherry 19 kirschrot
chest of drawers 33 Kommode
chest 16 Brust; 47 Truhe
child lock 49 Kindersicherung
child-safety catch 45 Kindersicherung
chimney 29 Schornstein
chip 40 schnitzeln
chlorofluorocarbon blown 57 FCK-Schaumstoff

cholesterol 18 Cholesterin
chopping blade 40 Schneidemesser
chrome 71 Chrom
circulation 16 Kreislauf
claim 59 behaupten
clarity 16 Klarheit
clash 32 nicht harmonieren, sich beißen
classic 11 klassisch
classical 22 klassisch
cleanser 54 Reiniger
clear 49 auf Null stellen
clearly 16 klar
cleated sole 8 Laufsohle
click on 95 klicken auf
click 67 Klicken
climbing 21t Bergsteigen
clockface 67 Zifferblatt
clockwise 16 im Uhrzeigersinn
close down 88t schließen
cloth 78 Stoff
club 23 Klub, Verein
clump 60 Klumpen
coated 8 imprägniert
coffee-maker 40 Kaffeemaschine
coil 35 Spirale
colourful 78 bunt, farbig
comb 56 Kamm
combination lock 24 Kombinationsschloss
combination 78 Kombination
combine 24 verbinden
comfort 35 Bequemlichkeit
commitment 75 Verpflichtung
common sense 75 gesunder Menschenverstand
communicate 84 sich verständigen
compact 40 kompakt
companion 76t Begleiter/in
company 27 Firma
complexion 54 Teint
complicated 30 kompliziert
comprehension 61 Verständnis
comprise 40 umfassen, bestehen aus
compromise 44 Kompromiss
conceal 40 verbergen
concrete 72 Beton
condition 58 Bedingung
cone spring 35 Sprungfeder
confidence 68 Selbstvertrauen
congratulations 14 herzlichen Glückwunsch
connect 38t verbinden
consider 35 erwägen
construction 35 Bau, Konstruktion
consult 18 konsultieren, sich wenden an
consumption 45 Verbrauch
contact 38t sich in Verbindung setzen mit
container 78 Behälter
contribute 16 beitragen
control trigger 71 Trigger
control 40 Regler
controller 78 Fernlenker

conventional 59 konventionell
cookbook 40 Kochbuch
cooking grid 71 Rost
cool 43 (ab)kühlen
coordination 14 Koordination
cope with 14 fertig werden mit
cord storage 40 Kabelfach
corded 72 mit Kabel
cordless 72 kabellos
corner block 35 Eckversteifung
cotton wool bud 54 Wattebausch
countryside 21t Landschaft
coupon 7 Gutschein
court shoe 8 Pumps
cover 32 Überzug
cow 58 Kuh
crash 94t abstürzen
cream 32 creme(farbig)
create 21t (er)schaffen
creativity 67p Kreativität
creature 51 Geschöpf
crime 70 Verbrechen
crockery 38t Geschirr
cross-country skiing 18 Skilanglauf
crowd 81 Menschenmenge
cruel 51 grausam
crumb tray 40 Krümelschale
cry 33 weinen
crystal balls 67p Kristallkugeln
crystal 43 Kristall
cuff links 65 Manschettenknöpfe
curler 56 Lockenwickler
current 49 augenblicklich, aktuell
curriculum vitae 88 Lebenslauf
curtain 30 Vorhang, Gardine
cushion 35 Kissen
cylinder cleaner 47 Bodenstaubsauger

D

damage 42 beschädigen
dancing 18 Tanzen
dangerous 42 gefährlich
day cream 50 Tagescreme
day off 13 freier Tag
deal, a great ~ of 67p eine Menge von
decibel 45 Dezibel
deck 35 Federung
decoratively 43 dekorativ
definition 85 Definition
delete 95 löschen
delicate 45 empfindlich
density 35 Dichte
deposit 28 Anzahlung, Kaution
depression 14 Depression
depth gauge 71 Tiefenmesser
describe 8 beschreiben
description 38 Beschreibung
design 21 entwerfen
dessert plate 38 Dessertteller
detachable 40 abnehmbar
detached house 28 freistehendes Haus
detail 19 Einzelheit, Detail
detective 81 Detektiv-

determination *68* Entschlossenheit
develop *14* entwickeln
device *40* Vorrichtung
diabetes *18* Zuckerkrankheit
diameter *38* Durchmesser
dictate *37* diktieren
diet *14* Ernährung
difference *23* Unterschied
digit *95* Ziffer
dinner plate *38* großer Teller
direction *16* Richtung
disaster *67p* Katastrophe
disc *40* Platte, Scheibe
discount *85* Rabatt
disease *60* Krankheit, Erkrankung
disgusting *62p* ekelhaft
dishwasher safe *40* spülmaschinenfest
display *49* Anzeige
dispute *67p* Auseinandersetzung
dissolve *43* (sich) auflösen
distribute *42* verteilen
dive *65* tauchen
divide *60* (sich) teilen
divorced *26* geschieden
DIY store *71* Bau-, Heimwerkermarkt
dizzy *16* schwindlig
DJ *18* Diskjockey
doctor *18* Arzt, Ärztin
doll's house *78* Puppenstube
doorbell *29* Türklingel
dowel *35* Dübel
drag *85* Belastung
drain *43* ablaufen lassen
drawcord *19* Kordelzugband
drawing *16* Zeichnung
dried-on *45* angetrocknet
drill *44* bohren
drip *31* tropfen
driving licence *25* Führerschein
drizzle *43* träufeln
dual-function *47* Doppelfunktion
durable *33* dauerhaft, haltbar
dust *44* Staub wischen
duty *75* Pflicht
dye *31* färben

E

ear *16* Ohr
ease *68* lindern
economy *45* Sparprogramm
education *90* Ausbildung
effect *60* (Aus-)Wirkung
eject *49* auswerfen
elasticated *19* elastisch
elbow *16* Ellbogen
electric *40* elektrisch
electronic *40* elektronisch
element *40* Element
embroidered *19* bestickt
emerald *67* Smaragd
emotion *68* Gefühl
employ *63* beschäftigen
employee *85* Angestellte/r
employer *85* Arbeitgeber/in

enamelled *71* emailliert
enclosure *91* Anlage
endless *75* endlos
energy *16* Energie
enhance *16* erhöhen, steigern
enormous *76t* enorm
entertain *78* unterhalten
envy *67p* Neid
equip *18* ausrüsten, ausstatten
equipment *18* Ausrüstung
equivalent *13* Entsprechung
erect *16* aufrecht
especially *45* besonders
even *14* sogar (noch)
evening class *21t* Abendschulkurs
evening course *21t* Abendkurs
evolution *60* Evolution
exciting *78* spannend
excluded *79* ausgeschlossen
exercise *13* trainieren; *14* körperliche Bewegung
exhausted *33* erschöpft
exotic *76* exotisch
expand *88* expandieren, vergrößern
expectation *44* Erwartung
experience *44* Erlebnis
expert *36* Experte/Expertin
expiry date *38* Verfallsdatum
explore *21t* erforschen, erkunden
explorer *78* Forscher/in
extend *45* verlängern
extra *35* zusätzlich
extract *34* Auszug
extremely *18* sehr, äußerst
eyeshadow *56* Lidschatten

F

face mask *54* Gesichtsmaske
facility *40* Vorrichtung
fact *78* Faktum
factor *18* Faktor
fail *22* scheitern
fair *63* fair, gerecht
fairly *75* ziemlich
familiar with, be ~ *85* sich gut auskennen mit
fare *83* Flug-, Fahrpreis
farmer *58* Bauer, Bäuerin
fashion design *21t* Modedesign
fashion *64* Mode
fast food *57* Schnellgerichte
fault *47* Defekt
fear *68* Angst, Befürchtung
feather *83* Feder
feeding bowl *76* Futternapf
feeling *21t* Gefühl
fence *29* Zaun
fertilizer *58* Dünger
field *58* Feld
fight *54* bekämpfen
finalize *74* endgültig festlegen
fine *81* Geldstrafe
finger *16* Finger
fit *19* passen (zu); Passform
flavour *43* Geschmack
fleece top *19* Fleeceshirt

flesh *62p* Fleisch
flexible *44* flexibel
flow *16* Zufluss, Fluss
fluent *88* fließend
fluid *15* Flüssigkeit
foam rubber *35* Schaumgummi
focus *16* konzentrieren
fold up *78* zusammenklappen
folding *40* zusammenklappbar
food processor *40* Küchenmaschine
food slicer *40* Allesschneider
fool *83* Narr/Närrin
forbidden *58* verboten
foretell *67p* vorhersagen
forgetful *75* vergesslich
fork *25* Gabel
formulate *54* formulieren
fortunately *55* glücklicherweise
frame *25* Rahmen
fray *35* abnutzen, ausfransen
frequent *54* häufig
frequently *75* häufig
friendly *63* freundlich
front door *29* Haustür
front *19* Vorder-
frying pan *40* Bratpfanne
full-time *44* Vollzeit-, Ganztags-
function *49* Funktion
furnish *78* möblieren
future *67p* Zukunft

G

garnet *67* Granat
gas central heating *28t* Gaszentralheizung
gate *83* Tor, Pforte
gauge *40* Anzeige
gear levers *25* Gangschaltung
GE *60* Gentechnik
gear *24* Gang
gemstone *64* Edelstein
gene *60* Gen
general *71* allgemein
genetic code *60* genetischer Code
gentle *54* sanft
give back *7* zurückgeben
give up *33* aufgeben
go off *69t* losgehen
goal *83* Tor
gold-plated *64* vergoldet
good, be ~ at sth *21t* gut in etw sein
gradually *14* allmählich, nach und nach
grain *54* Grain
graphite *23* Graphit
grass *30* Gras, Rasen
grater *40* Reibe
gravy boat *38* Sauciere
grip *40* Griff
guarantee *40* Garantie
guide *47* Führer/in
guinea-pig *51* Versuchskaninchen
gun *77* Pistole
gym teacher *33* Sportlehrer/in

H

haircut 33 Haarschnitt
half price, at ~ 11 zum halben Preis
hall 29 Flur, Diele
hammer/rotary drill 71 Schlagbohrer
hand-held 78 tragbar
handlebars 25 Lenker
hand-tied 35 handbefestigt
hang up 46 aufhängen
happiness 67p Glück, Fröhlichkeit
hardwood 35 Hartholz
head 16 Kopf
heading tape 34 Vorhangband
headlamp 25 Scheinwerfer, Lampe
headlights 78 Scheinwerfer
heal 43 heilen
hear 69t hören
heart disease 18 Herzkrankheit
heat 43 Hitze, Wärme
heating 28 Heizung
height 38 Höhe, Größe
helpless 44 hilflos
hematite 67 Hämatit
hen 58 Huhn
high performance 45 Hochleistungs-
high-heeled 8 Stöckel-
high-lift facility 40 Hebevorrichtung
highlight 47 hervorheben
hiking boot 8 Wanderschuh
hips 16 Hüften
history 68 Geschichte
hit 23 schlagen, treffen
hob 40 Herdplatte
hole 44 Loch
homonym 82 Homonym
honest 59 ehrlich
hooded 19 mit Kapuze
hoop earrings 65 Ohrreifen
hose 71 Schlauch
household chores 44 Hausarbeiten
household gadget 40 Haushaltsgerät
housework 44 Hausarbeit(en)
human 51 Mensch
hurry up 6 sich beeilen
hurt 9t (sich) wehtun, schmerzen
hyphen 37t Bindestrich
hypo-allergenic 64 anti-allergische
hypocritical 62p heuchlerisch

I

icing sugar 43 Puderzucker
icon 95 Symbol
ill 17 krank
illness 18 Krankheit
imagination 68 Vorstellungskraft
imagine 45 sich vorstellen
impatient 60 ungeduldig
import 76t importieren
impregnate 11 imprägnieren
improve 67p verbessern
in advance 14 im Voraus
in line with 16 in einer Linie mit
in stock 38t vorrätig

in the sale 6 reduziert
in vitro 51 im Reagenzglas
inactive 18 inaktiv
inactivity 18 Inaktivität
inch 24 Zoll
included 42 eingeschlossen, enthalten
incomplete 93 unvollständig
increase 14 steigern
independent 63 unabhängig
indicator 40 Anzeige
indoor court 23 Hallenplatz
indoors 21t innen
industry 77 Industrie
inexpensive 65 preiswert
influence 68 beeinflussen
inform 27 informieren, benachrichtigen
ingredients 55t Zutaten
injured 56 verletzt
in-line skating 13 Inlineskaten
inner 68 innere(r,s)
insect 59 Insekt
insert 49p einlegen
insole 8 Brand-, Einlegesohle
inspect 58 inspizieren
instance, for ~ 50 zum Beispiel
insurance 76t Versicherung
intellectual 14 intellektuell
intensify 67p verstärken
interior 45 Innere(s), Innenausstattung
intuition 68 Intuition
invite 62p einladen
invoice 92 Rechnung
involve 51 einschließen, umfassen
involved in 18 bezüglich
iron 44 bügeln
irritate 54 reizen
item 11 Artikel

J

jasper 67 Jaspis
jealous 68 eifersüchtig
jelly 43 Wackelpeter
jersey 19 Jersey
jet 45 Düse
jigsaw 71 Stichsäge
job centre 84 Arbeitsamt
job experience 90 Berufserfahrung
jogging 18 Jogging, Dauerlauf
join 23 beitreten
joint 18 Gelenk
journey 76t Reise
joy 67p Freude
joyful 68 freudig
junk food 14 minderwertiges Essen
just in case 38t nur für den Fall

K

keen on 21t wild auf
keep 30 behalten
kettle barbecue 71 Grillgerät
kettle 40 Wasserkocher
keyword 95 Stichwort
kid 84 Kind

kill 59 töten, umbringen
kiln-dried 35 im Ofen getrocknet
kitchen sink 45 Küchenspüle
knee 16 Knie
knee-high 8 kniehoch
kWh 45 Kilowattstunde

L

laces 8 Schnürsenkel
lace-up shoe 8 Schnürschuh
lack 68 mangeln an
ladder 72 Leiter
ladle 40 Schöpfkelle
lance 71 Lanze
landing 83 Gang (im oberen Stock)
landlady 30 Wirtin, Vermieterin
lane 28 Gasse, Weg
language 21t Sprache
lapis lazuli 67 Lapislazuli
laser pistol 77 Laserpistole
last 18 letzte(r,s)
latest 34 neueste(r,s)
laugh 33 lachen
lay 31 (ver)legen
lead to 14 führen zu
lead 71 Hundeleine
leaf 83 Blatt
league 21t Liga
leak 47 undichte Stelle
leatherware 11 Lederwaren
leave on 55t darauf lassen
left over 59 übrig geblieben
leg 16 Bein
lesson 23 (Unterrichts-)Stunde
level 18 Spiegel
lid 40 Deckel
lie 13 liegen
lift, give sb a ~ 7 jdn (mit dem Auto) mitnehmen
lightweight 23 Leicht-
likely 47 wahrscheinlich
lilac 19 lila
limescale 40 Kalkstein
line space 92 Leerzeile
line 46 (Wäsche-)Leine
lining 8 Futter(stoff)
lipstick 56 Lippenstift
listener 18 Zuhörer/in
listing 95 Eintrag
litter-box 76t Katzenklo
living room 32 Wohnzimmer
lizard 76t Eidechse
load 45 Ladung, Füllung
local 21t örtlich
lock up 58 einsperren
lock 24 abschließen
logic 67p Logik
logical 63 logisch
lonely 76t einsam
look after 14 aufpassen auf
look at 51 ansehen
lounge 28 Wohnzimmer, Salon
lower 18 senken
low-heeled 8 mit niedrigen Absätzen
luck 67p Glück

luggage carrier 24 Gepäckträger
lungs 18 Lungen
lycra 19 Lycra

M

madam 9t meine Dame
magnetic 78 magnetisch
mains power 72 Stromnetz
mains transformer 78 Stromtransformator
major 47 bedeutend
majority 59 Mehrheit
make friends 14 Freunde finden
make sb do sth 18 jdn dazu veranlassen/bringen, etw zu tun
make sure 49p sich vergewissern
manual work 85 Handarbeit
maple 35 Ahorn
masonry bit 71 Betonbohrer
masonry 72 Mauerwerk
match 21t Spiel
mature 63 reif
maximum 35 höchste/r/s
medical 76t medizinisch
medicine 50 Medikament(e)
meditation 68 Meditation
medium heel 8 halbhoher Absatz
mental 16 geistig
mercury 57 Quecksilber
mess around with 60 herumpfuschen
microwave oven 47 Mikrowelle
middle 10 Mitte
mid-sized 23 mittlerer Größe
milk pan 40 Milchtopf
mill 35 Spinnerei
minimum 45 minimal
minority 59 Minderheit
mirror 33 Spiegel
miss out on 21t verpassen
mobile phone stall 85 Stand für Mobilfunk
mobility 71 Beweglichkeit
modelling 78 Modellbau
moisturizer 54 Feuchtigkeitscreme
monster 77 Monster
moustache 36 Schnurrbart
move into 36 einziehen
move 16 Bewegung
mudguard 24 Schutzblech
mug 38 Becher(tasse)
mule 8 Schlappen
multi-purpose knife 40 Kombimesser
muscle 18 Muskel
mutation 60 Mutation
muzzle 76 Maulkorb

N

napkin 38 Serviette
nappa leather 33 Nappaleder
nasty 32 hässlich
natural 50 natürlich
nature 60 Natur
necessary 44 nötig, notwendig
necklace 64 (Hals-)Kette

need 14 Bedürfnis
neighbour 26 Nachbar/in
neither 90 keiner
neutralize 68 neutralisieren
news 17 Neuigkeit(en)
next to 10 (direkt) neben
nib 83 (Schreib-)Feder
nobody 28t niemand
noise 47 Geräusch
none 13 keine/r/s
non-iron 32 bügelfrei
non-meat 62p fleischlos
nonporous 18 nicht porös
non-slip 40 rutschfest
non-stick 42 teflonbeschichtet
nor 60 auch nicht, noch
not yet 28t noch nicht
notice 21t (be)merken
nowadays 44 heutzutage
nubuck 8 Nubukleder
number 78 Ziffer, Zahl

O

oak 35 Eiche
occasion 11 Anlass, Gelegenheit
ocean 34 Meer
odd 56 nicht passend
off-roader 78 Geländewagen
oil-free 54 fettfrei
oily 54 fettig
olive oil 55t Olivenöl
on test 46 im Test
on the one hand 52 einerseits
on the other hand 52 andererseits
one-handed 71 Einhand-
one-to-one 23 Einzel-
opal 67 Opal
opening 40 Öffnen
opera 22 Oper
operate 45 bedienen
operating instructions 49 Bedienungsanleitung
operation 45 Betrieb
opportunity 95 Gelegenheit
opposite 56 Gegenteil
opt 35 sich entscheiden
option 95 Option
order form 38 Bestellformular
order, place an ~ 38 eine Bestellung aufgeben, bestellen
organism 60 Organismus
organization 58 Organisation
organize 17 organisieren
out of stock 82 nicht vorrätig
outdoor court 23 Platz im Freien
outdoor 13 im Freien
outstretched 16 ausgestreckt
oval 38 oval
overdo 14 übertreiben
overdry 54 austrocknen
overpressure 40 Überdruck
overseas 76t Übersee
overweight 13 übergewichtig
own 75 besitzen
own, of one's ~ 28 eigen
own, on one's 42 allein

oxford (shoe) 8 geschnürter Halbschuh

P

pack of four 38 Viererpack
padded 8 gefüttert
padding 35 Polsterung
pain 18 Schmerz
paint 21 malen
painting 30 Malerarbeiten
palm 16 Handfläche
pamphlet 51 Broschüre
pan set 40 Kochtopfset
panel 49 Feld, Tafel
paragraph 83 Absatz, Abschnitt
parrot 76t Papagei
part-time 88 Teilzeit-
passionate 24 leidenschaftlich
past 69t an … vorbei
patent leather 8 Lackleder
patience 68 Geduld
patient 63 geduldig
payment 92 Bezahlung
peace 83 Frieden
peach 43 Pfirsich
pearl 65 Perle
pedal 25 Pedal
pendant 64 Anhänger
pepper mill 38 Pfeffermühle
per cent 6 Prozent
per week 28 pro Woche
perfect 19 vollkommen, perfekt
period 76t Zeit(raum), Zeitspanne
permanent 40 permanent
personnel manager 86 Personalchef/in
pessimism 63 Pessimismus
pesticide 58 Pestizid
petrol mower 71 Benzinmäher
photos, take ~ 21 fotografieren
physical 18 körperlich
pick out 32 aussuchen
pick 18 auswählen
picture 16 sich vorstellen
piece of advice 18 ein Ratschlag
pierce 64 lochen
pin 65 (Ansteck-)Nadel
pity, what a ~ 24 wie schade
place setting 45 Gedeck
plaster 36 Gips
plastic 78 Plastik
platform soled shoe 8 Schuh mit Plateausohle
platter 38 Platte
play on a team 21 in einer Mannschaft spielen
play 21 spielen
playback picture 49 Playbackbild
pleasant 18 angenehm
plenty of 9t eine Menge, viel
plug in 42 anschließen
pocket 19 Tasche
point out 47 hinweisen auf
point 16 Punkt; 60 Sinn
polar fleece 19 Thermofleece
policeman 70 Polizist

pollution *54* Verschmutzung
polystyrene foam *57* Polystyrol, Styropor
pony tail *36* Pferdeschwanz
pore *54* Pore
position *49p* Position
powder *43* Pulver
power drill *72* Elektrobohrer
powerful *68* stark
practise *22* (ein)üben
precious *68* Edel-
preferably *54* vorzugsweise
prepare *43* vorbereiten
prescription *83* Rezept
present *42* Geschenk
press and hold switch *40* Sicherheitsschalter
pressure washer *71* Hochdruckreiniger
prevent *16* (ver)hindern, verhüten
previous *47* vergangen
primarily *67p* vor allem, hauptsächlich
primary school *90p* Grundschule
priority *35* Vorrang, Priorität
prison *81* Gefängnis
prize *7* Preis
proceed *95* weitergehen
process *58* (weiter)verarbeiten
processed food *13* industriell hergestellte Nahrungsmittel
produce *60* produzieren
productivity *14* Produktivität
professional *23* Profi
profit *61* Profit
programme *60* programmieren
progress *45* Fortschritt/e
prompt *95* auffordern
prop stand *24* Fahrradständer
prosecute *81* strafrechtlich verfolgen
protect from *35* schützen vor
protect *40* schützen
protection *40* Schutz
protein *62p* Protein
prove safe *51* sich als sicher erweisen
prove *58* beweisen
provide *35* bieten, sorgen für
public limited company *92* Aktiengesellschaft
public transport *57* öffentliche Verkehrsmittel
pulse action *40* pulsierende/ stampfende Arbeitsweise
pump *25* Pumpe
punishment *35* starke Beanspruchung
purchase *95* (Ein-)Kauf
purify *67p* reinigen
put up *30* anbringen
puzzling *78* Puzzlespiel

Q

quality *35* Qualität
quantity *38* Menge
quick set recording *49* Aufnahme
quite a few *88t* eine ganze Menge

R

rabbit *51* Kaninchen
race *22* (Wett-)Rennen
racing car *77* Rennwagen
rail *34* Schiene
raise *62p* aufziehen
range *50* Sortiment
rank *47* einstufen
rapid *40* Schnell-
rational *68* rational
rayon *35* Kunstseide
razor *56* Rasierer
reach *81* nach etwas greifen
reaction *76t* Reaktion
ready-made *34* Fertig-
real *63* echt, wirklich
rear *25* Hinter(rad)-
reason *63* Vernunft, Grund
recharge *57* aufladen
recipient *67p* Empfänger/in
recycle *57* recyceln
reduce *11* reduzieren
reduction *21t* Ermäßigung
reference number *38* Bestellnummer
reflector *25* Rückstrahler
refrigerate *43* kühlen
refuse *21t* ablehnen, sich weigern
regards, with best ~ *92* Viele Grüße
regular *14* regelmäßig
regularly *13* regelmäßig
relationship *44* Beziehung
relax *14* (sich) entspannen
release *40* freisetzen
reliable *47* zuverlässig
rely on *46* sich verlassen auf
remain *54* bleiben
remains *58* Rückstände
reminder *27* Mahnung
remote control handset *49* Fernbedienung
removable *40* abnehmbar
remove *32* entfernen, abziehen
require *18* benötigen, erfordern
reset *49* zurückstellen
resilience *35* Elastizität
resist *60* widerstehen
resistance *68* Widerstand
resistant *56* strapazierfähig
responsibility *75* Verantwortung
responsible *63* verantwortlich
retailing *85* Einzelhandel
reverse *44* umkehren
revolution *72* Umdrehung
rewind *49* zurückspulen
ride *24* fahren (mit)
right *23* genau
rim *25* Felge
ring up *9t* anrufen
rinse off *54* abspülen
rinse *55t* spülen
rise *86* (Gehalts-)Erhöhung
risk *18* Risiko
risky *60* riskant
rock crystal *67* Bergkristall
role *44* Rolle

rope *72t* Seil
rubber backing pad *71* Gummipolster
rubber *8* strapazierfähig
rubberized *18* gummiert
ruby *67* Rubin
run around *58* herumrennen
rust-free *45* rostfrei

S

sad *33* traurig
saddle *25* Sattel
safety pressure valve *40* Überdruckventil
safety *92* Sicherheit
salad bowl *38* Salatschüssel
salary *85* Gehalt, Lohn
salt mill *38* Salzmühle
sandal *6* Sandale
sanding disc *71* Schmirgelscheibe
sapphire *67* Saphir
satin *34* Satin
satisfied *7* zufrieden
saucepan *40* Kochtopf
saucer *38* Untertasse
sb is likely to do sth *18* jd wird etw wahrscheinlich tun
scientist *60* (Natur-)Wissenschaftler/in
scissors *56* Schere
scores *14* Punkt(estand)
scratchpost *76* Kratzbaum
scream *69t* Schrei
screw *35* schrauben
screwdriver *72t* Schraubenzieher
scrub *54* Gesichtspeeling
sea salt *55t* Meersalz
seat *9t* (Sitz-)Platz
secondary school *90p* höhere Schule
secret *55* Geheimnis
secretary *28t* Sekretär/in
section *49p* Abschnitt
secure *24* sicher
select *49* auswählen
self-sufficient *75* autark
selling *88* Verkauf
semi-detached house *28t* Doppelhaushälfte
semi-final *22* Halbfinale
semi-precious *68* Halbedel-
sense *63* Sinn, Gefühl, Empfindung
sensitive *50* empfindlich, sensibel
serious *14* schwer, ernsthaft
serious, be ~ about *17* etw im Ernst tun wollen
serving dish *43* Servierschüssel
set *67* (ein)stellen
settle in *88t* sich zurechtfinden
sew on *44* annähen
sew *21* nähen
sexual *67p* sexuell
shackle lock *24* Bügelschloss
shade *32* (Farb-)Ton
shape *14* Form, Verfassung
share *28* (sich) teilen, gemeinsam nutzen

sharp 40 scharf
sheep 78 Schaf
sheet 83 Blatt (Papier)
shield 71 (Schutz-)Schild
shift 75 Schicht
shipping 95 Versand
shoplifter 81 Ladendieb(in)
shopping cart 95 Einkaufswagen
shove 81 stoßen
shred 40 zerkleinern
side effect 61 Nebenwirkung
sieve 40 Sieb
sight 49 Sicht
silly 61 töricht
single 16 einzeln
skating 18 Eislauf
ski 11 Ski
skin type 54 Hauttyp
skin 50 Haut
skincare product 54 Hautpflegeprodukt
sleeping basket 76 Schlafkörbchen
sleeve 19 Ärmel
slice 40 schneiden
slicing 40 Schnittstärke
slide 40 gleiten
slightly 54 leicht
slim 36 schlank
sling back shoe 8 Slingbackschuh
slip-on shoe 8 Slipper
slow down 16 langsamer werden
smelly 75 stinkend
smoker 63 Raucher/in
snake 76t Schlange
social 14 sozial, gesellschaftlich
society 75 Gesellschaft
sofa bed 32 Sofabett
soil 58 Erde
sort 75 Art
space invader 77 Angreifer aus dem Weltall
space 58 Raum
spade 71 Spaten
spare time 21 Freizeit
specification 35 Vor-, Angabe
speed 16 Geschwindigkeit
spend 21t verbringen
spill 55 verschütten
spin 16 (sich schnell) drehen
spinal fluid 16 Rückenmarksflüssigkeit
spinal 16 Rückgrat-
spine 16 Rückgrat
spiritual 67p geistig
sponge cake 43 Biskuitkuchen
sports 19 Sport-
sportswear 19 Sportkleidung
spot 54 Pickel
spread 55t streichen, verteilen
spring 83 (Sprung-)Feder
square inch 35 Quadratzoll
square metre 58 Quadratmeter
squeeze 78 drücken
staff 84 Mitarbeiter/innen
stain 32 Fleck
stainless steel 40 rostfreier Stahl

stain-repellent 35 schmutzabweisend
stand 16 stehen, sich hinstellen; 38 Tablett
starve 60 (ver)hungern
state 92 angeben
stay with 18 bleiben bei
step 23 Schritt
sterling silver 64 Sterlingsilber
stiletto heel 8 Pfennigabsatz
still picture 49 Standbild
stimulate 78 anregen
stir 43 (um)rühren
stomach 16 Magen
straight away 9t sofort
strap 6 Riemen
strappy shoe 8 Riemchenschuh
strength 35 Stärke
strengthen 18 stärken
stressed 68 gestresst
strict 58 streng
strike 94t Streik
stripe 32 Streifen
strong 24 kräftig (gebaut)
stud earrings 65 Ohrstecker
study 21t lernen, studieren
stuff 51 Zeug
stupid 81 dumm
sturdy 78 stabil
styling 24 Gestaltung
subject line 91 Betreffzeile
submit 95 unterbreiten
substance 58 Substanz, Stoff
subtotal 38 Zwischensumme
succeed in 21t gelingen
suddenly 69t plötzlich
suede 7 Wildleder
suffer 47 leiden
sunblock 56 Sonnenschutz
supper 69t (das) Abendessen
supply 71 liefern
support 35 Halt
suppose 52 glauben, vermuten, denken
suppress 67p unterdrücken
surface 43 Oberfläche
surrounding 24 umgebend, umliegend
survey 47 Umfrage
survive 76t überleben
sweat 19 Schweiß
sweaty feet 84 Schweißfüße
swimming 18 Schwimmen
switch off 49 ausschalten
switch on 49 einschalten
switch to 49 umschalten auf
symbolize 68 symbolisieren
synonym 62 Synonym
synthetic 8 synthetisch

T

tab 95 Feld
tableware 38 Tafelgeschirr
tab-top 34 Schlaufe
tag 35 Etikett
tank top 19 Pullunder

tap 31 Wasserhahn
tape counter 49 Bandzähler
tape 19 Band
teacher 27 Lehrer/in
team 21 Mannschaft
teapot 38 Teekanne
tear 83 zerreißen
tears, in ~ 81 in Tränen aufgelöst
teaspoon 55t Teelöffel
technical 77 technisch
technique 23 Technik
technology 24 Technik, Technologie
teen 54 Teenager
telly 69t Fernseher
tennis whites 23 weiße Tenniskleidung
tense 14 angespannt, nervös
tension 68 Spannung
terrible 17 schrecklich, furchtbar
test 13 prüfen, testen, (aus)probieren
tester 50 Probe
textile 22 Textilie
than 13 als
theft 24 Diebstahl
thick 40 dick
thief 81 Dieb/in
thigh 16 (Ober-)Schenkel
thin 40 dünn
thorough 55t gründlich
thought 67p Gedanke
thrilling 21t aufregend
throughout 68 überall (in), die ganze Zeit hindurch
tie clip 65 Krawattenspange
tie-back 34 Raffhalter
tighten 54 festigen
time, take up ~ 75 Zeit verbrauchen
toasting chamber 40 Toastkammer
toddler 78 Kleinkind
toe cap 8 Schuhkappe
toe 8 Spitze; 16 Zehe
toiletries 57 Toilettenartikel
tolerance 68 Toleranz
tolerant 76t tolerant
tongue 8 Zunge
tool kit 71 Werkzeugkasten
tool 40 Werkzeug
topaz 67 Topas
top-class performance 45 hervorragende Leistung(en)
total 38 Gesamt(preis)
toucan 78 Tukan
tough 40 robust
tourist attraction 78 Touristenattraktion
tournament 23 Turnier
track 78 Rennstrecke
tracksuit 19 Jogginganzug
tradition 63 Tradition
transaction 95 Geschäft
transparent 67p durchsichtig
tread 23 Profil
treat 35 behandeln
treatment 33 Behandlung

trial period 85 Probezeit
trifle 43 Biskuit-Nachspeise
trip 24 Ausflug, Fahrt
triple 40 dreifach
truth 59 Wahrheit
try out 25 (aus)probieren
turn down 49 leiser stellen
turn into 30 (sich) verwandeln in
turn on 44 einschalten
turner 40 Wender
turns, take sth in ~ 9 etw abwechselnd tun
turtle 76t Wasserschildkröte
TV, watch ~ 13 fernsehen
twinkling 78 glitzernd, flimmernd
typical 78 typisch
tyre 25 Reifen
T-zone 54 T-Bereich

U

ugly 30 hässlich
ultimate 23 allerletzte/r/s, allergrößte/r/s
unable 44 unfähig, nicht in der Lage
unauthorized 95 unbefugt
underweight 13 untergewichtig
unemployed 26 arbeitslos
unfurnished 30 unmöbliert
unloved 44 ungeliebt
unnecessary 57 unnötig
unplug 41 den Stecker herausziehen
unscramble 15 in die richtige Reihenfolge bringen
unusual 47 ungewöhnlich
up to 6 bis zu
upholstered 35 gepolstert
upper 8 Oberteil
upright cleaner 47 Handstaubsauger

V

vacant 86 frei
vaccination 76t Impfung
vaccine 60 Impfstoff

vacuum 46 (staub)saugen
vacuum-cleaning 44 Staubsaugen
valance 34 Volant
vanilla 43 Vanille
variable 40 verstellbar
vary 24 sich unterscheiden, variieren
VCR 47 Videorekorder
vegetarian 62p Vegetarier/in
veggie 62 Vegetarier/in
vehicle 78 Fahrzeug
vet(erinarian) 76 Tierarzt, -ärztin
vibrate 72 vibrieren
vice versa 44 umgekehrt
video game 81 Computerspiel
violent 77 gewalttätig
virtual 75 virtuell
vision 16 Blick
vitality 67p Vitalität
voicemail 94 Mailbox
volume 71 Volumen, Menge

W

wage 84 Lohn
wake up 69t aufwachen
walk, take a ~ 76t spazieren gehen
wall plug 71 Dübel
wall 44 Wand, Mauer
wallpaper 30 Tapete
war game 77 Kriegsspiel
ward off 67p abwehren
wardrobe 30 Kleiderschrank
warehouse 93 Lagerhaus
washable 19 waschbar
wash-dryer 47 Waschmaschine mit Trockenschleuder
washing-up 44 Abwasch
watchmaker 65 Uhrmacher/in
waterproof 8 wasserdicht
water-proofing 11 Imprägnier-
water-resistant 65 wasserdicht
wattage 72 Wattleistung
waxy 8 (wachs)weich

weakness 68 Schwäche
weather 18 Wetter
weave 35 weben
wedding ring 65 Ehering
wedge heel 8 Keilabsatz
weeds 59 Unkraut
weekly 85 wöchentlich
weigh 35 wiegen
weight 67p Gewicht
wellness 13 Gesundheit, Wohlbefinden
wet 42 nass, feucht
whenever 62p immer wenn
whip 43 schlagen
whisk 40 Schneebesen
white bread 13 Weißbrot
whole milk 55t Vollmilch
whole 19 ganze/r/s
wide fitting 8 bequem passend
width 34 Breite
win 21t gewinnen
wind forward 49 vorlaufen
winder 67 Aufzugsknopf
window sill 29 Fensterbrett
windsurfing 21 Surfen
wire 71 Draht
wisdom 67p Weisheit
wise 47 weise, klug
witness 70 70 Zeuge, Zeugin
wonderful 26 wunderbar, -voll
work overtime 85 Überstunden machen
working hours 28t Arbeitszeit
worried about, be ~ 33 besorgt sein um
worth 24 wert
wrapping 57 Verpackung
wrist 16 Handgelenk

Z

zebra 78 Zebra
zero 49 Null
zip fastening 19 mit Reißverschluss

Basic word list

Diese Liste enthält ca 900 Grundwörter, die in Shopping Matters 2 als bekannt vorausgesetzt werden. Nicht aufgeführt, jedoch vorausgesetzt, sind einige elementare Wörter, wie Präpositionen, Pronomen und Zahlen sowie Wörter, die im Englischen und Deutschen die gleiche Bedeutung haben, wie z. B. *hotel*, *radio* und *hobby*.

A

a bit recht, ziemlich
a long way ein weiter Weg
a lot viel, sehr
abbreviation Abkürzung
about über, ungefähr
above über, oben
accept annehmen, akzeptieren
accessory Accessoire
act out durchspielen
actually eigentlich
add hinzufügen
address Adresse
advertisement (ad) Anzeige
afraid, I'm ~ leider
after nach, nachdem
afterwards nachher, danach
afternoon Nachmittag
again wieder
age Alter
ago vor
agree übereinstimmen
air Luft
airport Flughafen
alarm clock Wecker
alcohol Alkohol
all alle
all right in Ordnung, (schon) gut
already schon, bereits
also auch, außerdem
always immer
American Amerikaner/in; amerikanisch
amount Summe, Betrag
animal Tier
answer Antwort; (be)antworten
any irgendetwas, irgendwelche(r/s); jede/r/s
any more nicht ... mehr
anyone jemand, jede/r
anything else sonst noch etwas
anyway jedenfalls
apologize sich entschuldigen
appliance Gerät
apricot Aprikose
around herum, ungefähr
arrive ankommen
article Artikel, Gegenstand
as wie, als
ask fragen, bitten
assistant Assistent/in
at night nachts
Austria Österreich
available erhältlich
awfully schrecklich

B

back zurück
bad schlecht, schlimm
band (Musik-)Kapelle
bank Bank, Ufer
battery Batterie
beautiful schön
because weil
become werden
bed Bett
before vor, vorher
begin anfangen
behind hinter, hinten
be interested in interessiert sein an
believe glauben
below unten(stehend)
big, bigger, biggest groß, größer, am größten
bill Rechnung
birthday Geburtstag
black schwarz
blackberry Brombeere
blue blau
body Körper
boil kochen
boot Stiefel
both beide
bottle Flasche
bowl Schüssel
box Kiste, Karton
boy Junge
branch Filiale
brand Marke
bread Brot
break zerbrechen
breakfast Frühstück
bright leuchtend, hell
bring (mit)bringen, holen
British britisch
brown braun
building Gebäude
bus Bus
business correspondence Geschäftsbriefe, Handelskorrespondenz
busy beschäftigt
button Knopf
buy kaufen
by um, von, durch

C

cake Kuchen
call (an)rufen
can dürfen, können
car Auto
cardigan Strickjacke
care Pflege
care for gerne haben
careful vorsichtig
carpet Teppich
carrier bag Tragetüte
carrot Karotte, Möhre
carry tragen
cash Bargeld
cashier Kassierer/in
cat Katze
catalogue Katalog
catch erreichen, nehmen
certain sicher, gewiss, bestimmt
certainly bitte schön
chain Kette
change Wechsel-, Kleingeld; umsteigen
cheap billig
check kontrollieren, (über)prüfen
checkout Kasse
chemist Apotheke
chicken Huhn, Hähnchen
child, children Kind, Kinder
chips Pommes frites
chocolate Schokolade, Praline
choose wählen, aussuchen
Christmas Weihnachten
cigarette Zigarette
clean reinigen; sauber
clever geschickt gemacht, klug
clock Uhr
close schließen
clothes Kleidung, Kleider
clothing Kleidung, Kleider
club Klub, Verein
coffee Kaffee
cold kalt
colleague Kollege, Kollegin
collection Kollektion
colour Farbe
come kommen

come on beeil dich, los
comfortable bequem
common gemeinsam
compare vergleichen
complaint Beschwerde, Klage
complete vervollständigen, ergänzen; vollständig
completely völlig
complimentary close Schlussformel
computer Computer
contain enthalten
cook Koch, Köchin; kochen
cooker Herd
copy abschreiben, kopieren
corner Ecke
correct richtig, korrekt; korrigieren
cosmetics Kosmetik(a)
cost Kosten; kosten
cotton Baumwolle
couch Couch
could konnte/n, könnte/n
country Land, Staat
couple Paar
couple, a ~ of ein paar, einige
credit card Kreditkarte
cube Würfel
cup Tasse
curly lockig
curtains Vorhänge
cushion Kissen
custard Vanillesoße
customer Kunde, Kundin
cut (zer)schneiden
cycling Radfahren

D

daily täglich, Tages-
damp feucht
dark, darker dunkel, dunkler
date Datum
day Tag
dear liebe/r
decide (sich) entscheiden
decision Entscheidung
deep tief
delay Verspätung
deli counter Feinkoststand
deliver liefern
delivery Lieferung
department Abteilung
describe beschreiben
design Muster; entwerfen
desk (Schreib-)Tisch, Schalter
dessert Nachspeise, Dessert
detergents Reinigungs-, Waschmittel
dialogue Dialog
dictionary Wörterbuch
different verschieden
difficult schwer, schwierig
dirt Schmutz
dirty schmutzig
dish Gericht
dishwasher Geschirrspüler
do tun, machen
dog Hund

doll Puppe
done getan; gar
double Doppel-
down (nach) unten, herunter
drainpipe Röhrenhosen, Abflussrohr
draw zeichnen
dream Traum; träumen
dress dekorieren; Kleid
drink trinken; Getränk
drive (Auto) fahren
drop fallen (lassen)
dry trocken; trocknen
dry-clean chemisch reinigen
during während

E

each jede/r/s
early, earlier früh, früher
earn verdienen
earring Ohrring
easy einfach, leicht
eat essen
egg Ei
Egypt Ägypten
either entweder
electrical elektrisch
elegant elegant
empty leer
end Ende
ending Ende (der Geschichte)
English Englisch
enjoy genießen, gern haben/tun
enough ausreichend, genug
envelope (Brief-)Umschlag
environmentally friendly umweltfreundlich
escalator Rolltreppe
etc usw.
ever je(mals), schon (ein)mal
every jede/r/s
everybody jede/r
everyone jede/r
everything alles
exactly genau
example Beispiel
excerpt Auszug
exercise Übung
exercise book Übungsbuch
expect erwarten
expensive teuer
expiry date Verfall(sdatum)
express ausdrücken

F

fabric Stoff
face Gesicht
false falsch
family Familie
famous berühmt
far weit (entfernt)
fashion boutique Modeboutique
fast schnell
favourite Lieblings-
feature Merkmal
feed füttern
feel (sich) fühlen, der Meinung sein

few ein paar, wenige
fill füllen
finally schließlich, zum Schluss
find finden, suchen
fine schön
finish (be)enden, aufhören (mit); Appretur
first erste/r/s, zuerst
fish Fisch
fit passen
fitness centre Fitnesscenter
fix reparieren
flat Wohnung
floor Etage, Stockwerk
flour Mehl
flower Blume
follow folgen
food Essen, Nahrung, Lebensmittel
foot Fuß
football Fußball
foreign Auslands-, ausländisch
forget vergessen
form Form; formen
free kostenlos, frei
free range Freiland-
freezer Gefrierschrank, Tiefkühltruhe
fridge Kühlschrank
friend Freund/in
from von, aus
fruit Obst, Frucht
full voll, vollständig
fun Spaß
funny lustig
furniture Möbel
further weitere/r/s

G

game Spiel
gap Lücke
garden Garten
garnish garnieren
gas Gas
get bekommen
gift Geschenk
gift wrap als Geschenk verpacken
give geben
glass Glas
glasses Brille
glue Klebstoff
good gut
goods Ware(n)
great toll, prima
green grün
grey grau
ground floor Erdgeschoss
group Gruppe
grow wachsen
guitar Gitarre
guy Kerl, Typ

H

hairdresser Friseur, Friseuse
hair-dryer Fön
half Hälfte; halb
hand Zeiger, Hand
handle anfassen, berühren

happen passieren
happy glücklich, zufrieden
hard schwierig, hart
hardly kaum
hardly ever fast nie
hate hassen, gar nicht mögen
have haben
health Gesundheit
healthy gesund
heavy schwer
help Hilfe; helfen
here hier
high hoch
high heel hoher Absatz
hold halten
holiday Ferien, Urlaub
home Zuhause, Heim
hope Hoffnung; hoffen
hospital Krankenhaus
hot heiß, warm
hour Stunde
house Haus
housewife Hausfrau
housing Wohnungen
how wie
hungry hungrig
hurry sich beeilen

I

idea Idee
identify erkennen
important wichtig
impulse Impuls
including inklusive
information Auskunft, Information(en)
in front of vor
ingredient Zutat
initials Initialen
inside innen
install installieren, einbauen
instead anstatt
instruction Anweisung
interesting interessant
interview Interview; interviewen
into in … hinein
iron Bügeleisen
Italian Italienisch
Italy Italien
item Artikel, Gegenstand, Ding

J

jewellery Schmuck
job (Arbeits-)Stelle, Beruf
juice Saft
just einfach, nur, bloß, gerade

K

key Schlüssel; Taste
kind Art
kitchen Küche
know kennen, wissen

L

label Etikett
lady Dame

lamp Lampe
large, larger groß, größer
late spät
lately in letzter Zeit
later später
law Gesetz
layer Schicht
layout Layout
learn lernen
least am wenigsten
leather Leder
leave abfahren, verlassen
left übrig; links
lemon Zitrone
lend leihen
length Länge
less weniger
let erlauben, (zu)lassen
letter Brief
letterhead Briefkopf
life Leben
lift Fahrstuhl
light leicht; Licht
like mögen, gern haben
liking Geschmack
limited company Gesellschaft mit beschränkter Haftung (GmbH)
line Linie, Zeile, Leine
linen Leinen
list Liste
listen zuhören
litre Liter
little klein, wenig
live wohnen, leben
long lange
look schauen, (aus)sehen
look for suchen
look forward to sich freuen auf
loose weit (geschnitten)
lose verlieren
loud laut
love lieben, sehr gern mögen
lovely schön, hübsch
low niedrig
luggage Gepäck
lunch break Mittagspause

M

machine Maschine, Gerät
magazine Zeitschrift
main Haupt-, wesentlich
make machen
make up erfinden, sich ausdenken
man, men Mann, Männer
manage (es) schaffen
manager Filialleiter/in, Chef/in
many viele
map Landkarte
mark Zeichen
market Markt
married verheiratet
mash Kartoffelpüree
match zuordnen; (zusammen) passen
material Stoff
matter Sache; etw ausmachen

may dürfen, können
maybe vielleicht
meal Essen
mean bedeuten
measure messen
meat Fleisch
medium mittlere/r/s, mittel-
meet treffen, kennen lernen
member Mitglied
menu Speisekarte, Menü
message Nachricht
method Methode
might könnte(n) (vielleicht)
milk Milch
minute Minute
miss verpassen
mistake Fehler
mix mischen
mixture Mischung
mobile phone Handy, Funktelefon
model Modell
month Monat
more mehr
morning Morgen
most am meisten
mountain (größerer) Berg
much viel
music Musik
must müssen

N

navy Marine
nearly fast
neck Hals
need brauchen
negative Verneinung; negativ
nephew Neffe
never nie(mals)
new neu
newspaper Zeitung
next nächste/r/s, danach
nice schön, nett
niece Nichte
night Nacht
normal normal
not nicht
note Note, Schein; Notiz
now nun, jetzt
number Zahl, Ziffer, Nummer
nurse Krankenpfleger/in
nylon Nylon

O

occur geschehen
October Oktober
off frei
offer anbieten
office Amt, Büro
often oft, häufig
old, older alt, älter
once (wenn) einmal
only nur
onto auf
open öffnen; offen
opinion Meinung
opposite gegenüber(liegend)

BASIC WORD LIST

order Bestellung; bestellen
ordinary gewöhnlich
organic organisch
organically grown organisch angebaut
other andere/r/s
out aus
outfit Ensemble, Kleidung
outside außerhalb (von)
over (vor)über
own eigene/r/s

P

packaging Verpackung
packet Päckchen, Paket
pair Paar
pale hell; blass
paper Papier, Zeitung
parents Eltern
partner Partner/in
party Party
past nach
pause Pause
pay (be)zahlen
payment Bezahlung
pen Stift
people Leute
perhaps vielleicht
pet Haustier
phone Telefon; anrufen
picture Bild
piece Stück, Blatt
place Platz; erteilen
plan Plan; planen
plane Flugzeug
plant Pflanze; pflanzen
please bitte
polite höflich
polyester Polyester
poor schlecht, mangelhaft
possible möglich
postcode Postleitzahl
pot Kanne
potato Kartoffel
pot plant Topfpflanze
poultry Geflügel
pound Pfund (Sterling)
pour gießen
power Energie
practice Übung, Training
prefer lieber mögen
pressure cooker Schnellkochtopf
pretty hübsch
price (Kauf-)Preis
probably wahrscheinlich
problem Problem
product Produkt
promise versprechen
properly richtig, korrekt
pull ziehen
purse Portemonnaie
put setzen, stellen
puzzle Rätsel

Q

quarter Viertel
question Frage

quiet ruhig, leise
quite ziemlich, ganz

R

rack Stange
racket Schläger
rather ziemlich
reach erreichen
read lesen
really wirklich, eigentlich
receipt Quittung, Beleg
receive bekommen
recipe (Koch-)Rezept
recommend empfehlen
red rot
reduced reduziert
reference (ref) Zeichen, Bezug
related verwandt
remember sich erinnern
rent Miete; mieten
repair reparieren
reply antworten
rest Rest
restaurant Restaurant
return zurückgeben, -kehren
rewrite umschreiben
right rechts, richtig; Recht
ring klingeln, läuten; Ring
roof Dach
room Raum, Zimmer
routine Routine
rug Vorleger, Teppich
run laufen; leiten, führen

S

safe Safe, Tresor
sale Verkauf
salutation Anrede
same gleiche/r/s, der-, die-, dasselbe
sausage Wurst
save sparen
say sagen
scarf Schal
scratch kratzen
season Jahreszeit
second zweite/r/s
see sehen
seem (er)scheinen
sell verkaufen
send schicken
sensible vernünftig
sentence Satz
separate andere/r/s
set Satz
several einige, mehrere
shampoo Shampoo
shelf Regal, Ablage
sherry Sherry
shirt Hemd
shoe Schuh
shoe polish Schuhcreme
shoe shop Schuhgeschäft
shop Laden, Geschäft
shop assistant Verkäufer/in
shop window Schaufenster
shoplifter Ladendieb/in

short, shorter kurz, kürzer
shorten kürzen
shorts kurze Hose
should solle/n, sollte/n
shoulder Schulter
side Seite
signature (block) Unterschrift(sabschnitt)
silk Seide
silver Silber
similar ähnlich
simple einfach
since seit
size Größe
sleep schlafen
slice Scheibe
slow, slowly langsam
small, smaller klein, kleiner
smart schick
smile lächeln; Lächeln
smoke rauchen
so also, damit
soap Seife
sofa Sofa
soft drinks alkoholfreie Getränke
sole Sohle
solution Lösung
solve lösen
some einige, etwas
someone jemand
something etwas
sometimes manchmal
song Lied
soon bald
sorry traurig
sound (sich) anhören, klingen
soup Suppe
spare übrig haben
speak sprechen, reden
special besondere/r/s
spell buchstabieren
spend ausgeben
spin-dry trockenschleudern
spoon Löffel
sport Sport(art)
sporty sportlich
spray Spray
stairs Treppe
standard normal
start anfangen; Beginn
stay bleiben, übernachten
steal stehlen
stew Eintopf(gericht); schmoren
still (immer) noch
stock auffüllen
stone Stein
stop anhalten, aufhören
store lagern; Laden
story Geschichte
stress Stress
student Schüler/in, Student/in
style Stil
subject Thema
such solch, so
sugar Zucker
suggest vorschlagen

suit stehen, passen
suitable passend
summer Sommer
sun Sonne
Sunday Sonntag
suntan lotion Bräunungslotion
supermarket Supermarkt
supply liefern; Lieferung
sure sicher
sweet Bonbon; süß
synthetic synthetisch
system System

T

table Tabelle, Tisch
tablecloth Tischdecke
tablespoon Esslöffel
take nehmen, dauern
talk Gespräch; reden
tall groß
taste kosten, probieren
teacher Lehrer/in
teacup Teetasse
telephone Telefon
television Fernsehen, -seher
tell sagen, erzählen
temperature Temperatur
tennis Tennis
tent Zelt
textiles Textilien
them ihnen, sie (3. Person Plural)
then dann
there da, dort, dorthin
these diese
thing Sache, Ding
think denken, meinen
those jene
through durch ... hindurch, durch
ticket (Fahr-)Karte
tight eng
tights (eine) Strumpfhose
till bis
time Zeit
times mal
tin Dose
toaster Toaster
together zusammen
tomorrow morgen

too zu
top oberer Teil, oberste/r/s
town Stadt
toy Spielzeug
traditional traditionell
train trainieren
trainee Auszubildende/r, Praktikant/in
trainers Turnschuhe
translation Übersetzung
transport Verkehr(smittel)
trip Reise
true richtig
try versuchen
tube Tube, Schlauch
tumble-dry (im Trommeltrockner) trocknen
tumble-dryer Trommeltrockner
turn abbiegen, (sich) umdrehen
turquoise türkis
TV-set Fernsehgerät
twice zweimal
type tippen

U

under unter
underground U-Bahn
understand verstehen
unfortunately leider
unmarried unverheiratet
until bis
upstairs oben
use benutzen
useful nützlich
usually normalerweise, gewöhnlich

V

various verschiedene
VAT MWSt
vegetables Gemüse
very sehr
video Video(film)
video camera Videokamera

W

waist Taille
wait warten
walk Spaziergang; (zu Fuß) gehen

want wollen
wash (sich) waschen
washing machine Waschmaschine
watch beobachten; (Armband-)Uhr
water Wasser
way Weg, Art, Weise
wear tragen, anhaben
website Webseite
week Woche
well gut, also
what was, welche/r/s
wheel Rad
when wenn, als, wann
where wo, wohin
whether ob
which welche/r/s
while Weile
white weiß
who wer, der/die/das
why warum
will werde(n)
win gewinnen, siegen
window Fenster
wine Wein
winter Winter
wish wünschen; Wunsch
with mit, bei
without ohne
woman Frau
woodwork Werken (mit Holz)
wool Wolle
word Wort
work Arbeit; arbeiten, funktionieren
world Welt
worse schlechter, schlimmer
would würde, würdest, würden
wrap (ein)wickeln
write schreiben
wrong falsch, unrecht

YZ

year Jahr
yellow gelb
young, younger jung, jünger
Yours faithfully Mit freundlichen Grüßen
Yours sincerely Mit freundlichen Grüßen

Additional vocabulary

Autozubehör	Car accessories
Abblendschalter	dimming switch
Auspuff	exhaust
Benzin	petrol
Blinker	indicator light
Bodenteppich	carpeting
Bremsflüssigkeit	brake fluid
Dieselöl	diesel oil
Gaspedal	accelerator
Heckscheibe	rear window
Kfz-Werkstatt	garage
Kofferraum	boot
Kontrolllampe	warning light
Kühler	radiator
Kupplung	clutch
Lenkrad	steering wheel
Luftfilter	air filter
Motor	engine
Motorhaube	bonnet
Reserverad	spare wheel
Rückspiegel	rear-view mirror
Schalter	switch
Scheibenwischer	windscreen wiper
Stoßstange	bumper
Tachometer	speedometer
Tankstelle	petrol station
Treibstoff	fuel
Türgriff	door handle
Türschloss	door lock
verstellbare Kopfstütze	adjustable headrest
Windschutzscheibe	windscreen
Zündschloss	starter

Babyartikel	Nursery ware
Babyautositz	baby carrier
rückwärts gerichtet	rear facing
Babybadewanne	baby bath
Babykörbchen und Ständer	moses basket and stand
Babyschuhe	bootees
Babytragetasche	carrycot
Babywippe	bouncing cradle
Baldachin	canopy
Bauklötze	building bricks
Beißring	teething ring
Flaschenwärmer	bottle warmer
Fußsack	foot muff
Gitterbett	cot
Häubchen	hood
Hemdchen	vest
Kindersitz	child seat
vorwärts gerichtet	forward facing
Kinderstuhl	high chair
Kinderwagen	pram
Lätzchen	bib
Laufstall	play pen
Matratze	mattress
Milchflasche	feeding bottle
Rassel	rattle
Sauger	teat
Schlafsack	sleeping bag
Schnuller	dummy
Sicherheitsgitter	safety barrier
Sportwagen	push chair
Strampelhose	leggings, rompers
Stubenwagen	bassinet, wicker pram
Töpfchen	baby's pot, potty
Wegwerfwindeln	disposable nappies
Wickelkommode	changing unit
Wickeltischaufsatz	changing top
Wiege	cradle
Windelhose	rubber baby pants
Windeln	nappies

Eisenwaren und Werkzeuge	Hardware and tools
Bandsäge	bandsaw
Bügelsäge	hacksaw
elektr. Bohrmaschine	electric drill
Feile	file
Fuchsschwanz	hand saw
Kneif-, Beißzange	pincers
Kombizange	all purpose pliers
Körner	centre punch
Kreuzschlitzschraubendreher	Phillips screwdriver
Laubsäge	fretsaw
Lötpistole	soldering gun
Meißel	chisel
Nägel	nails
Raspel	rasp
Rohrzange	pipe wrench
Schrauben	screws
Schutzbrille	goggles
Vibrationsschleifer	orbital sanding attachment
Wasserwaage	spirit level
Werkzeugkasten	tool box
Zollstock, Maßstab	folding rule

Elektrische Haushaltsgeräte	Electrical household articles
Bügelsohle	sole plate
Bügeltisch	ironing table
elektr. Bügelautomat	electric ironing machine
elektr. Bügeleisen	electric iron
elektr. Kaffeemühle	electric coffee grinder
elektr. Warmhalteplatte	electric hot plate
Elektroherd	electric cooker
Fleischwolf	mincer, food chopper
Griff	handle

136

Grill	rotisserie
Grillspieß	spit
Handrührgerät	hand mixer
Kühlschrank	refrigerator, fridge
Staubsauger	vacuum cleaner
Tauchsieder	immersion heater
Toaster	toaster
Waffelautomat	electric waffle iron
Wäscheständer	airer
Waschmaschine	washing machine
Waschtrommel	washing drum
Zitronenpresse	lemon squeezer

Fotografie	Photography
Adapterring	adapter ring
Auslöser	shutter release
Belichtungsmesser	exposure meter
Bildfenster	film window
Blitzlampe	flash head
Blitzlicht	flash
Blitzschalter	flash switch
Digitalkamera	digital camera
Einstellscheibe	focusing screen
Entfernungsskala	distance scale
Fernglas	binoculars
Fischauge	fisheye
Kameratasche	camera case
Kassettenkamera	cartridge-loading camera
Kleinbildkamera	miniature camera
Kleinbildkassette	miniature film cassette
Messgeräte	meter
Objektiv	lens
Rückspulkurbel	rewind handle
Schraubdeckel	screw-in cover
Stativ	tripod
Teleobjektiv	telephoto lens
Weitwinkelobjektiv	wide-angle lens
Würfelblitz	flash cube
Zubehörschuh	accessory shoe
zweiäugige SpiegelReflexkamera	twin-lens reflex camera

Geschirr und Küchengeräte	Tableware and kitchen utensils
Dessertlöffel	dessert spoon
Flötenkessel	whistling kettle
Gemüseschüssel	vegetable dish
Kochlöffel	wooden spoons
Kochtopf	(cooking) pot
Korkenzieher	corkscrew
Kuchenform	cake tin
Salatbesteck	salad servers
Salatschüssel	salad bowl
Sauciere	sauce boat, gravy boat
Serviettenring	serviette ring
Stielkasserolle	saucepan
Suppenterrine	soup tureen
Thermoskanne	thermos jug
tiefer Teller	deep plate, soup plate
Vorlegebesteck	serving cutlery

Haustiere	Pets
beißen	bite
Bulldogge	bulldog
Dackel	dachshund
Deutscher Schäferhund	German shepherd
Fell	coat
getigert, gestreift	tabby
Goldfisch	goldfish
Hamster	hamster
Kanarienvogel	canary
kastriert	castrated
Kater	tom cat
Katzenjunges	kitten
Landschildkröte	tortoise
Männchen, männlich	male
Meerschweinchen	guinea pig
Mischung	mongrel
Pfote	paw
Pudel	poodle
Rauhhaar	wired coat
Salzwasserfisch	saltwater fish
Stammbaum	pedigree
sterilisiert	sterilized
Süßwasserfisch	freshwater fish
Tierfutter	pet food
Wachhund	watchdog
Weibchen, weiblich	female
Wellensittich	budgie, budgerigar
Welpe	puppy
Züchtung	breed
Zwerghase	dwarf rabbit

Kosmetikartikel	Cosmetics
Augenmake-up-Entferner	eye make-up remover
Badesalz	bath salt(s)
Bürste	brush
Feuchtigkeitscreme	moisturising cream
Haarbalsam	hair conditioner
Haarspray	hair-spray
Handcreme	hand cream
Kondome	condoms
Monatsbinden	sanitary towels
Nachtcreme	night cream
Nagellackentferner	nail polish remover
Puderdose	powder tin
Rasierwasser	aftershave lotion
Reinigungsmilch	cleansing lotion
Rouge	blusher
Schaumbad	foam bath
Tagescreme	day cream
Tampons	tampons
Zahnbürste	toothbrush
Zahnpasta	toothpaste

Kurzwaren, Accessoires	Haberdashery, accessories
Fäustlinge	mittens
Fingerhut	thimble
Garn	thread
Gürtel	belt
Häkelnadel	crochet hook
Häkelarbeit	crochet
Handarbeiten	needlework
Handschuhe	gloves
Hut	hat
Knopf	button
Knüpfarbeit	knotted work
Maßband	tape measure
Mütze, Haube	cap

Nadelkissen	pincushion
Nähen	sewing
Nähgarnrolle	cotton reel
Nähnadeln	needles
Reißverschluss	zip (fastening)
Sonnenbrillen	sunglasses
Spitzen	laces
Stickerei	embroidery
Stricknadeln	knitting needles

Lederwaren, Schuhe	Leatherware, shoes
Aktentasche	briefcase
Beuteltasche	dolly bag
Brieftasche	wallet
Einkaufstasche	shopping bag
Freizeitschuhe	casual shoes
Geldbörse	purse
Gepäckset	luggage set
Hausschuhe	slippers
Kappe	counter
Keil, Zwickel	gusset
kleine Handtasche	purse bag
Koffer	suitcase
Kosmetikkoffer	vanity case
Regenstiefel	wellingtons
Reisetasche	travel bag
Samt	velvet
Skischuhe	skiing boots
Seesack	duffle bag
Umhängetasche	shoulder bag
Umschlag (Stiefel)	collar
Umschlag, Hülle	case, jacket
Wanderschuhe	hiking boots
zehenfreie Sandalen	peep toe sandals

Möbel	Furniture
Couchtisch	coffee table
Doppelbett	double bed
Esstisch	dining table
Frisierkommode	dressing table
Garderobenwand	coat rack
Kopfteil	headboard
Küchenschrank	kitchen cupboard
Nachttisch	bedside table
Polsterelementgruppe	upholstered suite
Polstersessel, Fauteuil	armchair
Schrank	cupboard
Schublade	drawer
Sideboard, Anrichte	sideboard
Stuhl	chair
Wandverbau	wall units

Papier- und Schreibwaren	Stationery
Bleistift	pencil
Block	writing pad
Bogen, Blatt	sheet (of paper)
Briefumschlag	envelope
Buntstifte	coloured pencils
Dreieck	triangle
Durchschreibepapier	carbon paper
Farbstift	crayon
Feder	(pen) nib
Federtasche	pencil case
Filzstift	felt pen, felt tipped pen
Füllfeder(halter)	fountain pen
Heft	exercise book, notebook, copy book
Heftklammer	staple
Heftmaschine	stapler
Klebeband	adhesive tape
Klebstoff	adhesive, glue
Lineal	ruler
Locher	punch, perforator
Mappe	folder
Mine	cartridge, refill
Ordner	briefcase, files
Patronen	cartridges
Pinsel	(paint) brush
Radiergummi	rubber
Reißzwecke	drawing pin, thumb tacks
Schultasche	satchel, school-bag
Spitzer	pencil sharpener
Stempel	stamp
Stempelkissen	ink-pad
Tagebuch	diary
Tinte, Tusche	ink
Wasserfarben	water colours
Winkelmesser	protractor
Zeichenblock	sketch pad
Zirkel	(pair of) compasses

Radio, Fernsehen, Unterhaltungselektronik	Radio, television, electronics
aufladbare Batterien	rechargeable batteries
Autoradio mit Recorder/ CD-Player	combination unit
Batterieladegerät	charger
Bildschirm	screen
Buchse	socket
Camcorder	camcorder
CD-Spieler	compact disc player
Doppelkassettendeck	twin cassette deck
Empfänger	receiver
Faxgerät	fax machine
Fernsehgerät	TV-set
Fernsehkanal	channel
halbautomatisch	semi-automatic
Kassettenbox	cassette storage, cabinet
Kassettenrecorder	cassette recorder
Kopfhörer	headphones, earphones
Lautsprecher	speaker, loudspeaker
Lautstärkeregler	volume control
Mobiltelefon, Handy	mobile phone
Plattenteller	turntable
Schallplattenspieler	record player
Spur	track
Stereoanlage	stereo system
Verstärker	amplifier
Videorecorder	video recorder
Walkman	Walkman®, personal stereo

Computerzubehör	Computer accessories
Bildschirm	screen
CD-Brenner	CD-burner/CD-writer
Drucker	printer
Farbdrucker	colour printer
Kabel	cable
Laufwerk	drive

Lautsprecher	speaker
Maus	mouse
Mauspad	mousepad
Speicher	memory
Tastatur	keyboard

Schmuck und Uhren	Jewellery and watches
Brillant	diamond
Brillantschliff	brilliant cut
Digitalanzeige	digital readout, light emitting diode (LED)
elektronische Armbanduhr	electronic wristwatch
Elfenbein	ivory
Gravur	engraving
Halsreif	choker, collar, neckband
Kettenglied	link
Kronenaufzug	winding crown
Ohrgehänge	pendant earrings
Pendel	pendulum
Quarz	quartz
Sanduhr, Eieruhr	hourglass (egg-timer)
Schließe	clasp
Schmuckgarnitur	set of jewellery
Schmucksteinanhänger	gemstone pendant
Standuhr	grandfather clock
Trauring(e)	wedding ring(s)
Uhrgehäuse	clock case
Uhrwerk	clockwork
Weißgold	white gold
Zuchtperlen	cultured pearls

Souvenirs	Souvenirs
Abzeichen	badge
Ansicht	view
Ansichtskarte	picture postcard
Anstecknadel	pin
Aufkleber	sticker
beleuchtet	illuminated
Beleuchtung	illumination
Bonbonniere	box of chocolates
Briefmarke	stamp
Brieföffner	letter opener
Brieftasche	wallet
Fahne	flag
Flaschenöffner	bottle opener
illustriert	illustrated
Kalender	calendar
Keramik	ceramics, pottery
Korkenzieher	cork screw
Kristall	crystal
Mandeln	almonds
Marzipan	marzipan
Mütze, Haube	cap
Nougat	nougat
Nüsse	nuts
Porzellan	porcelain
Pralinen	chocolates
Puppe	doll
Schal	scarf
Schnaps	strong liquor, schnapps
Spielkarten	playing cards
Süßwaren	confectionery
Tagebuch	diary
Tracht	national costumes
vergoldet	gold plated

Spielwaren	Toys and games
Ankleidepuppe	fashion doll
Brettspiele	board games
Buchse	socket
Computerspiele	computer games
Damespiel	draughts
Domino	dominoes
Dreirad	tricycle
Gesellschaftsspiele	party games
Knetmasse	modelling clay
Kreativspiele	creative games
mechanischer Baukasten	construction set
Mensch-ärgere-dich-nicht	ludo
Mikroskopausrüstung	microscope kit
Plüschtier	soft toy
Queue	cue
Schach	chess
Schaukelpferd	rocking horse
Spielemagazin	compendium of games
Spielkarten	playing cards
Spielknüppel	control stick
Spielstein	piece, counter
Traktor und Anhänger	tractor and trailer
Verbindungskabel	linking cable
Würfelbecher	dice cup
Würfelspiel	dice

Sport- und Campingartikel	Leisure and Camping Goods
Ausrüstung	equipment
Badeanzug	bathing suit
Badehose	bathing trunks
Campingliege	camp bed
Eislaufen	ice-skating
Eislaufschuhe	ice-skates
Federball	shuttlecock
Federballspiel	badminton
Gaskocher	gas cooker
Hängematte	hammock
Hauszelt	ridge tent
Holzkohle	charcoal
Klappstuhl	folding chair
Lagerfeuer	camp fire, bonfire
Langlaufen	cross-country skiing
Luftmatratze	airbed, lilo
Matte	mat
Netz	net
Petroleumlampe	storm lantern
Rennbahn	race track
Rodel	toboggan
Rollschuhe	roller skates
Rucksack	rucksack, backpack
Sattel	saddle
Schistöcke	poles
Schlafsack	sleeping bag
Schnorchel	snorkel
Sporthalle	gym, gymnasium
Springschnur	skipping rope
Steilwandszelt	frame tent
Surfbrett	surfboard
Taucherbrille	diving goggles
Tischtennisschläger	table tennis bat, paddle
Torstange	goalpost
Wohnwagen	caravan
Zelthering	tent peg

Zeltleine	guy	Rollo	blinds
		Rüschen	frills
		Schaffell	lambskin
Teppiche, Tapeten, Vorhänge	**Carpets, wallpaper, curtains**	Schlingflor	loop pile
		schmutzabweisend	dirt resistant
Bodenbelag	floor covering	selbstklebend	self-adhesive
Bordüre	border	Spitzenvorhang	lace curtain
Fliesen	tiles	Tapeten	wallpaper, wallcoverings
Fransen	fringes	Teleskopstangen	tension rods
geknüpft	knotted	Vorhänge	curtains
Haken	hooks	Vorhangstangen	curtain poles
handgewebt	handwoven	Vorleger, Teppich	rug
Hochflorteppich	shag pile carpet	Vorhangschiene	curtain rail
Jalousie	Venetian blind	Webeteppich	woven carpet
Orientteppich	oriental carpet		

Common irregular verbs

be	was/were	been	sein
become	became	become	werden
begin	began	begun	anfangen
bring	brought	brought	bringen
buy	bought	bought	kaufen
catch	caught	caught	fangen
choose	chose	chosen	wählen
come	came	come	kommen
cost	cost	cost	kosten
do	did	done	tun, machen, erledigen
drink	drank	drunk	trinken
drive	drove	driven	fahren
eat	ate	eaten	essen, fressen
feel	felt	felt	(sich) fühlen
find	found	found	finden
forget	forgot	forgotten	vergessen
go	went	gone	gehen
get	got	got	bekommen, erhalten
give	gave	given	geben
have	had	had	haben
hear	heard	heard	hören
hold	held	held	halten
keep	kept	kept	behalten
know	knew	known	kennen, wissen
learn	learnt/learned	learnt/learned	lernen
leave	left	left	verlassen
lend	lent	lent	verleihen
let	let	let	lassen
lose	lost	lost	verlieren
make	made	made	machen
mean	meant	meant	bedeuten
meet	met	met	sich treffen
pay	paid	paid	(be-)zahlen
put	put	put	setzen, stellen, legen
read	read	read	lesen
ring	rang	rung	klingeln, anrufen
run	ran	run	laufen
say	said	said	sagen
see	saw	seen	sehen
sell	sold	sold	verkaufen
send	sent	sent	senden, schicken
sit	sat	sat	sitzen
sleep	slept	slept	schlafen
speak	spoke	spoken	sprechen
spend	spent	spent	ausgeben, verbringen(Zeit)
stand	stood	stood	stehen
steal	stole	stolen	stehlen
take	took	taken	nehmen
teach	taught	taught	unterrichten, lehren
tell	told	told	erzählen, mitteilen, sagen
think	thought	thought	denken, meinen
understand	understood	understood	verstehen
wake	woke	woken	wecken
wear	wore	worn	tragen
write	wrote	written	schreiben

Quellenverzeichnis

Grafiken
Oxford Designers & Illustrators

Fotos
A. Austin: S. 74 (3); **Bosch**: S. 40 (5), 47, 71(4); **CeDe Futtermittel GmbH**: S. 71; **Jan Chipps Photography**, London: S. 4 (4), 5, 6, 8, 9, 24, 30, 32, 50, 77, 84; **Christ**: S. 65 (5); **COMSTOCK**, Luxemburg: S. 4, 13 **Corbis Stockmarket**, Düsseldorf: S. 21/T. Stewart/C&B productions/C. Keeler jr.; **Das Fotoarchiv**, Essen: S. 14/Eisermann, 17/Eisermann, 21/Oberhäuser, Tack (2), Hollenbach, Weller, 55+106/Tack; **U. Diekmann**: S. 5, 65 (5); **Fissler**: S. 40 (2); **Gardena**: S. 4, 71; **Gedore Werkzeugmaschinen**: S. 71; **Geowissenschaftliche Sammlung, Berkakademie Freiberg**: S. 67/A. Massanek; **Greenpeace Fotoarchiv**, Hamburg: S. 58/ Morgenstern /Steche; **GRUNDIG**: S. 47 (2); **F. Hübner.**: S. 78 (2); **KAHLA/Thüringen Porzellan GmbH**: S. 4, 39; **MATTEL/Fisher Price**, Dreieich: S. 78 (4); **NIKE International**: S. 19; **pwe Kinoarchiv**, Hamburg: S. 70; **Scalextric**: S. 78 ; **SIEMENS**: S. 45, 47 (6); **Sportimage**, Hamburg: S. 23/Action Images/Bob Martin; **STOCKFOOD**, München: S. 43, 71; **M. Strecker**: S. 4, 21, 53, 60, 74 (2); **TEFAL**: S. 40 (2); **John Walmsley**, Guildford: S. 21;

Wir danken folgenden Firmen für die freundliche Unterstützung:
Robert BOSCH Hausgeräte GmbH, München
CeDe Futtermittel GmbH
CHRIST Juweliere und Uhrmacher, Dreieich
Fissler GmbH, Idar-Oberstein
Gardena Holding AG, Ulm
Gedore Werkzeugmaschinenfabrik, Remscheid
GRUNDIG AG, Nürnberg
KAHLA/Thüringen Porzellan GmbH, Kahla
MATTEL GmbH für Fisher Price, Dreieich
NIKE International, Mörfelden
Scalextric
SIEMENS Haushaltgeräte GmbH, München
TEFAL, Offenbach

Nicht alle Copyright-Inhaber konnten ermittelt werden; deren Urheberrechte werden hiermit vorsorglich und ausdrücklich anerkannt.